Watches

The Ultimate Guide

In memory of my father, Jean.

© 2010 Assouline Publishing
601 West 26th Street, 18th floor
New York, NY 10001, USA
Tel.: 212 989-6810   Fax: 212 647-0005
www.assouline.com

ISBN: 978 2 7594 0416 2
Color separation: Gravor (Switzerland) and Planète Couleurs (France)
Printed in Italy

First published in 2006.
Translated from French by Nicholas Elliott for the Art of Translation,
with additional translations by Scott de Lesseps and Leah Brumer.

Fabienne Reybaud

Watches
The Ultimate Guide

ASSOULINE

Montre-Bracelet, by César Baldacchini, 1987. Compression, Unikat.
15.7 inches x 7.8 inches x 7.8 inches. Galerie Carzaniga, Bale.

Table of Contents

Introduction

The Watch Phenomenon
Once upon a time, the watch was a little box with a dial and a mechanical movement inside it. People carried this little box with them to tell time. Today it only takes a glance at a computer, a cell phone, or even the door of a microwave to know what time it is—competition is stiff. The time is everywhere. And the clever inventors of all these high-tech modern machines predicted the death of the watch.

Yet man is a strange animal, with a curious preference to hold on to his old ticker, the mechanical secrets of which his forbears labored over for ten centuries, rather than look at the timer on his washing machine. Today, about two billion watches are sold each year, sixty-three watches per second, for an overall turnover of $55 billion. Under the guidance of Switzerland, which earns more money from the export of watches than any other country, the watch industry has experienced a spectacular transformation over the last twenty years. Not only have the Swiss succeeded in rehabilitating "old-fashioned" technical know-how in the era of quartz (which is far more accurate),

Dali What Makes You Tick?, Philippe Halsman, 1953.

PATEK PHILIPPE
GENÈVE

but, above all, they have managed to make the watch's actual function entirely superfluous.

When Swiss watch exports passed the historic 17 billion Swiss franc benchmark in 2008, the Swiss watch industry federation crowed, "We sell dreams." When it auctioned a Patek Philippe for more than 4 million Swiss francs, or well over $2.5 million, in April 2004, setting a world record for a steel watch, the Christie's auction house in Geneva proclaimed, "We sell art." And when it introduced the most complicated wristwatch in the world in 2005 after ten thousand hours of development work for its 250th anniversary, Vacheron Constantin explained, "We sell know-how." Collectors are unanimous: They aren't buying time, but pleasure. For the cogs of these small objects now spin to the rhythm of desire: Desire to wrap a unique piece around your wrist, desire to let yourself be seduced by the new, desire, finally, to be reminded that watches demonstrate this simple precept that, "of all the arts, horology may be the one in which ignorance should least be tolerated."

66Of all the arts, watchmaking may be the one in which ignorance should be least tolerated.99

***Diderot and d'Alembert's* Encyclopedia**

PREVIOUS PAGES: (left) Detail of a hand-wound chronograph mechanism for a Vacheron Constantin watch. (right) Charlie Chaplin in *Modern Times,* 1936.

OPPOSITE: An advertising campaign for a Patek Philippe watch.

What Makes Watches Tick?

A watch contains a landscape of bridges, plates, and cogs —a constantly moving landscape—in which the cognoscenti can recognize the lunar phase, the solar time, or the beat of a tourbillon. It is a landscape of parts entirely invented by man, in his never-ending quest to master time. From the sundial to the quartz watch, the clepsydra to the pocket watch, civilizations throughout human history have attempted to divide time into increasingly fine, precise fractions. The following pages provide an overview of the tumultuous history of these astonishing machines to master time, along with an alphabetical glossary that sheds light on the mysteries of watchmaking jargon. Because before you choose a timepiece, you'd best know what it's made of.

Movement of an A. Lange & Söhne Langematik moon phase watch.

FIRST TIME

Once Upon a Time . . .

Egyptians of the Middle Empire called the first hour of sunlight "the brilliant hour," and the first hour of night "the defeat of the enemies of Re." In a bid to master fleeting hours, the Egyptians were the first time chasers to assign names to specific hours. By the Middle Empire, the people of the Nile had already adopted the twenty-four-hour day from the Sumerians. Next, Egyptian priests made the passage of time tangible by inventing the first elementary timepiece, the "shadow clock." Shadow clocks consisted of a long horizontal stem with an elevated crossbar aligned to the stars. Through arcane calculations, Egyptians were able to use this system to chart the passage of time. But the shadow clock was deemed too complex, and was soon replaced by the gnomon, a simple stick planted in the ground. As the earth rotated, the gnomon's shadow moved around a graduated surface, indicating the time of day. The sundial was a success for centuries: its era lasted four millennia, right until the early twentieth century, when it was still used to set clocks for railroad networks. There was just one little problem: the first universal time measurement device didn't work at night. The Egyptians responded by inventing the clepsydra (a name derived from the Greek for "water thief"), a graduated

Obelisk-shaped sundial (or gnomon) in the north arm of the transept of the Église Saint-Sulpice in Paris. Every day, when the sun reaches its highest point, sunlight passes through a lens in the stained-glass window of the south transept and hits the brass line. The distance from the point where sunlight hits the line to the obelisk varies according to the time of year.

93

PREVIOUS PAGES:
Leonardo da Vinci, *Manuscript L* 1497–1502; Fol 92 verso: astronomical clock dial on which the Sun and Venus appear. Fol 93 recto: text on firearms. Pencil and ink. H. 4.29 inches, W. 2.83 inches. Bibliothèque de l'Institut de France, Paris.

OPPOSITE: Turkish market pocket watch, circa 1800. Dial with Turkish numerals; movement by Edward Prior, London. International Museum of Horology, La Chaux-de-Fonds.

RIGHT: (top) Portrait of Dutch physicist Christiaan Huygens (1629–1695), drawing by Édouard Garnier.
(bottom) Portrait of Swiss watchmaker Abraham-Louis Breguet (1747–1823).

and pierced container filled with water. The gradual release of water from the container made it possible to measure the passage of time. But although accurate, clepsydras weren't of much use if there was a frost. And since sundials didn't work when it rained, it was time to find something new. It would take tens of centuries for the rhythm of human life to escape the yoke of shadow, sun, water, sand, or oil (certain oil lamps could tell time). Though it first appeared in the eleventh century, the clock did not become truly prevalent until two centuries later. The clock's inventor may be lost in the mists of time, but his invention met with early praise. Everyone agreed from the beginning that this new instrument, made of metal cogs and weights, had a distinct advantage over its rudimentary predecessors: its mechanism told time consistently, all the time. Consistent but often imprecise, these early monumental clocks were used to mark the time for prayer and frequently ran up to an hour late. The invention of the spring motor and fusee systems in the late fifteenth century lightened the clock's movement by ridding it of its reliance on weights. Then, in 1675, Dutch physicist Christiaan Huygens revolutionized the measurement of time by inventing the balance hairspring, a minuscule part that reduced time gains and losses to a few minutes a day.

The bulky, full-sized clock soon developed into the mantel clock, which in turn led to the watch. Public and religious time became private, domestic time. In 1690 the first minute hands appeared on thick,

Double-cased Turkish market watch with a chateleine, 1778–1779. Crafted by Georges Goodman, with agate, jasper, and gold, Louvre Museum, Paris.

Seventeenth-century round enamel watch with
apocryphal Breguet signature, Louvre Museum, Paris.

LEFT (clockwise from upper left): Two watches made by Abraham-Louis Breguet (with watch-maker Jean-Louis Joly), circa 1800–1802, silver, enamel, brass, and gold. H. 5.91 inches, W. 23.62 inches, Louvre Museum, Paris and souscription watch by Abraham-Louis Breguet, 1797–1805, movement, brass, gold (metal), and fine metalwork. H. 3.94 inches, W. 22.44 inches, Louvre Museum, Paris; military field watch with pedometer by Breguet and Son, 1800–1825, silver, movement, gold, and fine metalwork. H. 3.15 inches, W. 18.5 inches, Louvre Museum, Paris; circular watch with a miniature map of France on its back, given by Napoleon I to Prince Borghèse, Breguet and Son 1804–1814, steel, silver, enamel, movement, and gold, Château de Fontainebleau.

The Esmeralda, Constant Girard-Perregaux's most celebrated Tourbillon with Three Gold Bridges, 1889.
Pink gold hunter case sumptuously engraved with "CG" monogram.
Enamel dial. This watch was reportedly given to the president of Mexico in the late nineteenth century.

Untitled (Rolex watch),
by Andy Warhol, circa 1983.

OPPOSITE: November 24, 1927, *Daily Mail* advertisement vaunting the merits of the Rolex Waterproof Oyster wristwatch, following swimmer Mercedes Gleitze's successful crossing of the Channel while wearing a Waterproof.

Attestation

de l'enregistrement de la marque suisse N° 15468

e Bureau soussigné atteste qu'il a enregistré dans le registre suisse des marques, la marque est reproduite ci-dessous:

N° 154683.   Date de dépôt: 22 janvier 1955, 8 l
G. Léon Breitling S.A. Compagnie des Montres Breitling et Montbrillar
(G. Léon Breitling Ltd. Breitling and Montbrillant Watch Manufactory
place du Molard 6, Genève (Suisse). — Marque de fabrique et de commerc

Tous produits horlogers, montres, parties de montres, mouvemen
dr e de montres, boîtes de montres, étuis de montres et s'y rapportant.

V CARRERA PANAMERICANA
EQUIPO MEXICANO
PATROCINADO POR

Los Embotelladores
Autorizados de

Coca-Cola

en la
República

lavishly decorated pendant watches, enameled by the era's greatest painters, and totally irresistible to the European aristocracy. Around the same period, the English perfected the quarter repeater watch, which struck on demand and could therefore tell time during the night.

More than a century later, French watchmaker Jean-Antoine Lépine helped trim the watch down by picking up where his brother-in-law Pierre-Augustin Caron's research had left off. Though Caron's literary accomplishments under the pen name Beaumarchais overshadowed his talents as a watchmaker, timepiece devotees remember him as the man responsible for imagining "the double virgule escapement," a set of parts that

29

❝My mission is to kill time, while time's mission is to kill me. We murderers get along well together.❞

Emil Cioran

made it possible to get rid of more cumbersome components and obtain a smaller caliber. "Through this method, I can make watches as flat as is deemed suitable, watches flatter than ever before. This convenience comes without sacrificing any of the watch's grace." The modern watch had arrived, and the Age of Enlightenment took firm hold of it. Watches were no longer limited to telling time. They served as alarms, indicated the date and the day of the week, and sometimes even the lunar phase. Geneva, which was mobbed with Calvinist watchmakers fleeing France after the revocation of the Edict of Nantes in 1685, became famous for its watches. At the end of the eighteenth century, master watchmakers were constantly succeeding in increasing the precision of their handiwork. In 1801, Abraham-Louis Breguet invented the tourbillon (French for "whirlwind"), which further reduced positional errors. Yet at this stage, people were still carrying their watches in their pockets. The first wristwatches didn't appear until the beginning of the twentieth century, when, in 1904, Cartier realized Brazilian aviator Alberto Santos Dumont's dream of a watch that he could read without letting go of his plane's controls. Following its release, during the First World War French infantrymen began tying their pocket watches to their wrists with pieces of string. The ultimate goal was now within sight. Rolex soon launched the first wristwatch, "as reliable and accurate as a pocket watch." By the 1930s, people were finally looking to their wrists to tell time, and the race for the ultimate in accuracy had been launched. In 1968 the arrival of quartz checkmated the mechanical calibers of old. The Swiss watchmaking industry reeled from the blow, but soon recovered by specializing in luxury timepieces that soften the inexorable passage of time.

The Glossary

Sculptor Armand Fernandez, known as Arman (1928–2005), standing in front of one of his 'accumulations' at the Gare Saint-Lazare in Paris on July 22, 1985.

A

Alternation

Time taken by the balance to go from one point to the other. The balance of a classic watch movement oscillates at a rhythm of 18,000 alternations per hour. Leading watch brands offer movements oscillating at 28,800 or even 36,000 alternations per hour.

Annual calendar

A watch that displays the date and automatically adjusts from thirty-one-day months to thirty-day months. Its mechanism must be adjusted every year.

Automatic

Invented by Abraham-Louis Perrelet in the eighteenth century and later perfected by Abraham-Louis Breguet, the automatic watch is a mechanical watch that uses the effect of gravity to wind itself solely through the movement of its owner's arm. This "self-winding" or "perpetual" watch, as it was once known, recycles the energy in the movements of the human wrist, which moves between 7,000 and 40,000 times a day, to turn an oscillating component known as the rotor. The rotor transmits the motive power thus accumulated to the watch's mainspring. The ease of the automatic watch, which saved people the trouble of winding their timepieces every day, contributed to its success, though the automatic didn't truly take off until the twentieth century. Harwood and Leroy both marketed automatic windup movement before they were superceded by Rolex, whose 1931 Perpetual wristwatch considerably improved the automatic timepiece.

B

Back

The part of a watch that seals the case, on the reverse side of the dial. It can be screwed, to ensure the water resistance of a diving watch, or transparent, in order to display the mechanical movement of a model through glass.

Balance

The component responsible for regulating the operation of a mechanical watch. Because its oscillations regulate the movement of the watch's mechanism, the balance is responsible for a watch's degree of accuracy.

Barrel

A hollow cylindrical part containing the movement's mainspring. Its toothed rim transmits motive power to the gear train and sets it in motion. More simply put,

the barrel delivers the motive power necessary for the watch to function.

Bezel

A part fitted to the case to hold the glass in place. In order to mark times when practicing athletic activities such as scuba diving, the bezel can be graduated and movable ("turning bezel").

Bridge

A metallic part fixed to the main plate to form the movement's frame. The bridge's purpose is to hold the caliber's various components together.

C

Calendar watch

Calendar watches display the date and generally indicate the day of the month in an aperture.

Caliber

The caliber once described the dimensions and arrangement of the various parts of a movement. These dimensions were expressed in "lines," with each line representing 0.09 of an inch. Today the caliber is followed by a series of numbers and/or letters, and describes the watch's shape, origin, and the name of its manufacturer. By extension, in watch terminology it is synonymous with the "movement."

Case

The exterior part of a watch serves the same purpose as a car's body: to protect the motor—in this case the movement—from various types of damage (water, dust, humidity, impact, etc.).

Chamfer

To round the sharp edges of a watch's components, notably for aesthetic reasons. An *haute hor-logerie* piece's sharp edges are chamfered by hand.

Chiming repeater

A watch that strikes the quarter hours in three or four different pitches.

Chronograph

An additional mechanism that allows a watch to measure time intervals. The mechanism governs a chronograph hand (a sweep second hand) placed at the center of the dial. It can be started, stopped, or brought back to zero by pressing a push button on the side of the case. The sweep second hand makes a complete revolution in one minute. Auxiliary counters on the dial keep count of the number of revolutions, in minutes (thirty-minute counter), and often also in hours (twelve-hour counter). Ninety percent of chronographs currently manufactured are quartz chronographs that record elapsed time to one-tenth of a second. The only exception is the Microtimer, a digital chronograph accurate to one-one-thousandth of a second. The Microtimer was launched on the market by TAG Heuer in 2002. In 2005 the same company unveiled the Calibre 360, the first mechanical wrist chronograph to measure elapsed time to one one-thousandth of a second.

Chronometer

A watch certified for high accuracy and reliability by the Swiss Chronometer Control Board (Contrôle Officiel Suisse des Chronomètres, COSC). Watch and clock companies are free to submit their calibers to the COSC. To warrant being called chronometers, mechanical and quartz movements are respectively tested for fifteen and eleven days in various positions and temperatures. The COSC certifies roughly one million chronometers per year. Rolex watches claim two-thirds of the certifications delivered by this prestigious Swiss organization.

Complication

A watch is known as a "complicated watch" when it offers functions other than displaying hours, minutes, and seconds. These functions can be astronomical (phases of the lunar cycle; equations of time, date, sunrise and sunset), practical (chronograph, striking work, minute-repeating), or technical, to improve the watch's accuracy (initially, the tourbillon).Complications are modules added to a watch's movement. A complicated piece also implies a high degree of skill on the watchmaker's part, evidenced both in the manufacture of the caliber and the finish of the model.

Côtes de Genève

A decorative pattern found on certain watch parts (such as the bridges). The pattern consists of even, parallel ridges that give the parts a ribbed appearance.

Crown

The crown is a knob attached to the exterior of a watch's case. It serves to wind the movement of a mechanical watch or to set the time and date on automatic and quartz models. In waterproof watches, the crown is screwed on in order to better protect the mechanism.

D

Dead, or independent seconds

A mechanical watch's second hand that jumps from one second to the next in a noncontinuous manner. Its name comes from the fact that it can be stopped "dead," while the watch continues to run.

Dial

Whether it is made of metal, gold, carbon fiber, enamel, or mother-of-pearl, the dial's surface indicates the watch's various functions (hours, minutes, seconds, etc.).

Display

Time can be displayed via analog (hands moving around the dial) and/or digital means (numbers appearing in one or several apertures). These two types of display are used in both mechanical watches and quartz watches.

Dual time

Dual time watches simultaneously display the time in two different time zones. They are also known as GMT watches, referring to Greenwich Mean Time. Some models can display three time zones, often with city names shown as references.

E

Ébauche, or movement blank

An incomplete watch movement most frequently purchased from specialized suppliers by watch-manufacturing brands. The *ébauche* is a raw part that does not include any of the watch's regulating parts, nor its dials and hands.

Equation of time

The difference between mean solar time and legal time, which, depending on the time of year, can vary from −16 minutes to +14 minutes. The display of this variation on a watch is considered extremely complicated work mastered by few brands (those that have succeeded include Audemars Piguet and Vacheron Constantin).

Escapement

In a mechanical watch, the escapement's function is to convey the gear train's energy to the balance in order to make it oscillate. The quality of the escapement has a direct impact on the movement's accuracy and reliability.

F

Fly-back

The fly-back hand is a feature of certain chronographs. Initially devised for airplane pilots, it resets the chronograph's second hand to zero with a single push of a button, then immediately resumes movement for another elapsed time measurement. Without the fly-back function, the same operation would require three separate steps.

Fondation Qualité Fleurier

A new quality label launched in the fall of 2004 in Fleurier, Switzerland, by four watch manufacturers (Chopard, Parmigiani Fleurier, Bovet Fleurier, and Vaucher Manufacture). Open to all Swiss and European producers of mechanical *haute horlogerie* (high-quality timepieces with complicated work), this quality label opens new aesthetic and technical criteria for the certification of finished watches. As opposed to other certifications, the Fleurier label takes all the characteristics expected of a high-end watch into account: accuracy, durability, and quality of the aesthetic finish.

G

Glass

The glass protects the watch's dial. On antique watches, the glass is made of crystal, which is difficult to scratch but highly fragile. In the early 1940s, crystal was replaced by synthetic glass (Plexiglass), which is unbreakable but easily scratched. Today manufacturers use scratch-resistant mineral glasses. High-quality watches generally have a sapphire glass.

Grande sonnerie, or "great strike"

Considered a complicated watch, *grande sonnerie* repeater watches strike the hour and the quarter hour automatically, like a clock. And like the minute repeater, the *grande sonnerie* can repeat full hours, quarter hours and minutes on demand. As for the *petite sonnerie* ("small strike") watch, it only automatically chimes on the hour.

H

Hairspring

A small spring coiled into a spiral and fixed to the balance. Together, the hairspring and the balance are part of the mechanical watch's regulatory mechanism. In short, the hairspring is essential for a watch to function properly. Without the hairspring, accuracy is impossible. Invented in 1675 by Christiaan Huygens, this tiny metal wire has become a high stakes component in the twenty-first century, primarily because it is difficult and expensive to make, but also because ETA (Swatch Group) has monopolized the manufacture of hairsprings for the entire Swiss watchmaking business.

J

Jewel

Stones placed inside the watch's movement as bearings to reduce friction between the parts. Today they are nearly always synthetic.

Joint

Joints are used in water-resistant watches in order to make the case entirely hermetic. They are placed at every junction between the case and the back, the glass, the crown, and the pushbuttons. They can be made of rubber, nylon, silicone, or Teflon.

Jump hour

On a jump-hour watch, the hour appears in an aperture on the dial. The hour changes abruptly by a "jump" of the plate.

L

LCD
(Liquid Crystals Display)

A Liquid Crystals Display system. LCD rests on organic substances (liquid crystals) sealed between two glass plates and connected to the integrated circuit of a quartz watch. This type of display is used to tell time on digital watches.

M

Main plate

A metallic plate on which all the parts of the watch's movement are mounted.

Mainspring

A thin steel ribbon coiled inside the barrel. It provides the power necessary for the movement to operate. In general, the mainspring is designed to drive the watch for thirty-six to forty hours.

Manufacturer

From the Latin *manu factum*, meaning "handmade." In watchmaking, though there is no legal definition of what constitutes a watch manufacturer, a company can theoretically make use of the term if it is directly responsible for every step of a watch's production. In actuality, few companies are able to achieve this level of control.

Minute repeater

Once indispensable to tell time during the night, the minute repeater continues to strike the hours, quarter hours, and minutes on today's highly complicated watches. The main difficulty is in fitting musical hammers, gongs, and the related mechanisms inside a watch case. On mechanical watches, the gear train of the striking-work is set in motion when the bolt is activated with a push of the owner's nail. Once the bolt is liberated, a ridged wheel reads the requested time and sets off miniscule hammers that strike the gongs, creating different tones for the hours, the quarter hours, and the minutes. Patek Philippe is the model of excellence in minute repeater watches.

Moon phase

Though moon phase watches indicating the lunar month first appeared in the seventeenth century, they remain largely inaccurate. Synchronization with solar time is rife with problems. While the moon's revolution around the earth lasts 27.32505 days, the time elapsed from one full moon to the next (a synodic revolution) is of 29.53059 days. For the watch's rotational movement to accomplish an exact revolution, a very powerful gear train capable of rectifying the variation between the two is needed. In fact, the majority of moon phase modules are based on a lunar cycle simplified to 29.5 days. As a result, every three years the watch's lunar calendar can be up to one day behind the moon, and the watch must be adjusted by a watchmaker. Nonetheless, moon phase watches by certain brands (such as Patek Philippe, IWC, and Hermès) have managed to accurately follow moon phases for up to 122 years before a first, single-day adjustment was required.

Movement

Assembly of parts (winding and setting mechanisms, mainspring, gear train, escapement, regulator) that make up the mechanical watch and allow it to function. A simple mechanical movement contains 150 components, as opposed to the 300 or even 500 components found in a complicated caliber.

Oscillator

Like the pendulum or the balance, the oscillator is a device that generates oscillations, which divide time into equal units.

Pallet

An anchor-shaped steel or brass part found in the escapement of mechanical watches. The pallet serves to transmit the power necessary for the balance to move.

Perpetual calendar

A watch that automatically indicates the day, the month, the date, the year—including leap years— and often the moon phase. Perpetual calendar mechanisms are conceived and programmed according to the Gregorian calendar to run until March 1, 2100, at which point they will be off by a single extra day. A simple adjustment by a watchmaker will then allow any perpetual calendar watch to run accurately for the following four hundred years.

Poinçon de Genève

A certification established in 1886 by the state of Geneva to recognize the superior manufacture of certain watch calibers. Unlike the COSC, the Poinçon de Genève does not base itself on a movement's operation and functions, other than a few very precise requirements regarding materials, finishes, etc. The central requirement is that the movement must be assembled and set in Geneva by a Geneva-based company. Poinçon de Genève is a prestigious quality label, the privilege of a few *haute horlogerie* manufacturers (Vacheron Constantin...).

Power reserve

Power reserve is displayed on the watch's dial. It shows how long (in hours or in days) the model will run before it needs to be automatically or manually wound.

Q

Quartz

Launched in the late 1960s in Japan, the quartz watch movement is an electronic movement in which a quartz crystal oscillating 32,768 times per second serves as a regulator (a balance). In a quartz watch, power is generated not by a barrel (the motor component of a mechanical watch), but by a battery. The battery generates the power required for an integrated circuit to run, and the quartz regulates this power. Because they don't need to be wound, quartz watches are five hundred times more accurate and practical than mechanical and automatic watch movements. The quartz watch established its lasting supremacy by taking over the global watch market in less than a decade.

R

Rotor

Also known as the oscillating mass, this moving metallic part is shaped like a half moon and found in automatic watches. Placed at the back of the watch's mechanism, the rotor uses the motion of the wearer's wrist to automatically wind the barrel's spring.

S

Screws

There are about thirty screws in a simple mechanical watch movement, and over eighty in a complicated caliber. In high-end movements, steel screws are given a blued finish through a particular thermal treatment resulting in an ice blue color. This treatment is purely for aesthetic reasons.

Seconde foudroyante

A *seconde foudroyante,* or split-second, chronograph measures fractions of seconds. Also known as the *diablotine,* the *foudroyante* is a hand that revolves around the dial in four or five jumps per second. It provides an accurate time measurement to a fourth or a fifth of a second.

Skeleton

A watch is referred to as a skeleton watch when all the parts of the movement have been cut out or finely chiseled so that only the mechanism is visible. This type of work is more heavily dependent on a silver or goldsmith's craft than on actual watchmaking complications.

Split-time counter

A chronograph with two sweep second hands whose motions can be dissociated to allow for the measurement of intermediary times. While a classic chronograph's second hand stops, then starts again on demand, without taking account of the time it was immobilized, a split-time counter records the time elapsed while the second hand was stopped to allow for a time reading. The split-time counter chronograph makes it possible to measure as many intermediary times as one wishes over the course of a single event.

Sweep second hand

The second hand of a chronograph. The sweep second hand measures one-fifth of a second, one-tenth of a second, and, in some models, even one-one-thousandth of a second.

Swiss Made

A designation certifying a watch was made in Switzerland. According to the 1971 Swiss Made Ordinance, a watch is considered Swiss if 50 percent of the movement's components are Swiss, if the movement was assembled and cased in Switzerland, and if the final testing by the watchmaker was done in Switzerland. A quality guarantee (and hence a commercial asset) for moderately priced watches, Swiss Made is far from being unanimously embraced by *haute horlogerie* manufacturers. In actuality, a Swiss-Made watch can be largely made in Hong Kong.

T

Tachometer

An instrument for measuring speed. In watchmaking, the tachometer is a sports timer or a chronograph equipped with a divided dial displaying speed in miles per hour or another unit.

Tourbillon

Invented for pocket watches in 1801 by Abraham-Louis Breguet, this device eliminates position errors due to the effect of gravity when the watch is held in a vertical position. The tourbillon is a mobile cage, which holds the watch's bal-

ance and revolves once per minute. Under the effect of gravity, the centrifugal force produced by the rotation of the cage automatically stops the watch from being fast or slow. Considered the quintessence of the art of watchmaking, the tourbillon was long the exclusive domain of the great watch manufacturers. Today times have changed, and nearly every brand, no matter its quality, offers tourbillon watches—in most cases with tourbillons purchased from Swiss or Chinese subcontractors.

U

Ultrathin

Ultrathin: an ultrathin watch is a watch whose size and thickness have been reduced to an absolute minimum. Watchmakers consider the bulk of the work to be in the miniaturization of the parts, rather than in actual complicated watch work. In 1903, Jaeger-LeCoultre designed a 0.054 inches–thick movement, and claimed the title for the thinnest pocket watch movement in the world. In 1925, Audemars Piguet did Jaeger-LeCoultre one better with a movement 0.052-inches thick. The same year, Blancpain designed a wristwatch under 0.69 inches. In the 1940s and 1950s, Audemars Piguet and Vacheron Constantin each brought out a 0.06-inches manually wound caliber. Today ultra-thin watches remain the trademark of companies such as Piaget, which is responsible for the 1956 manual windup Caliber 9P (0.078 inches); the 1960 Caliber 12P, the thinnest self-winding watch in the world at 0.09 inches; and in 2003, the thinnest tourbillon movement (0.14 inches).

Water-resistant

The case of a water-resistant watch is designed to protect it from dust and water. Water-resistant models can withstand pressure of 3 to 5 bars at depths of 100 to 160 feet. Practically speaking, a water-resistant watch is safe from accidental encounters with water (rain, housework, splashes), but not from total immersion, intensive diving, and especially, deep sea diving. In these cases, it is best to opt for a watch tested at greater depths (330 to 660 feet), with a screwed crown and back.

The Art of Starting a Watch Collection

In 2008 the market for collectible watches generated about $265 million in sales, three times the amount it had generated in 2003. And despite the fall 2008 financial crisis, projections for 2010 stay optimistic. One can argue that the boom is related to the fact that watches, unlike paintings or cars, are intimate objects. Watches are not hung on walls, parked in garages, or lavishly enthroned in living rooms; they are worn on a daily basis. A watch follows its owner wherever he goes, immediately revealing to those in the know his taste, his financial means, and his understanding of the wheels of time. Serious watch collectors differ from art collectors in that they often fight an uphill battle to establish the object of their passion. Convincing your friends and family that it is of the utmost necessity for you to accumulate calibers that will indicate actual solar time and leap years until 2100, and strike quarter hours and minutes on demand, can be quite a challenge.

Only a collector understands that winding a watch that has required thousands of hours of precision work is pure, unadulterated pleasure. Only a collector knows that listening to the sound of a watch's crown as it is lovingly caressed, or observing the hypnotic oscillations of a movement, can have the effect of a powerful drug. And only a collector is convinced that, in a sense, the glory of owning something infinitely small makes us infinitely great.

Yet before you reach that point, you will have to get up to speed with a market where the worst sits next to the best, the fake is mixed with the authentic, and savage speculators rub shoulders with the most guilelessly sincere. The long and the short of it is that starting a watch collection is a treacherous, tricky business.

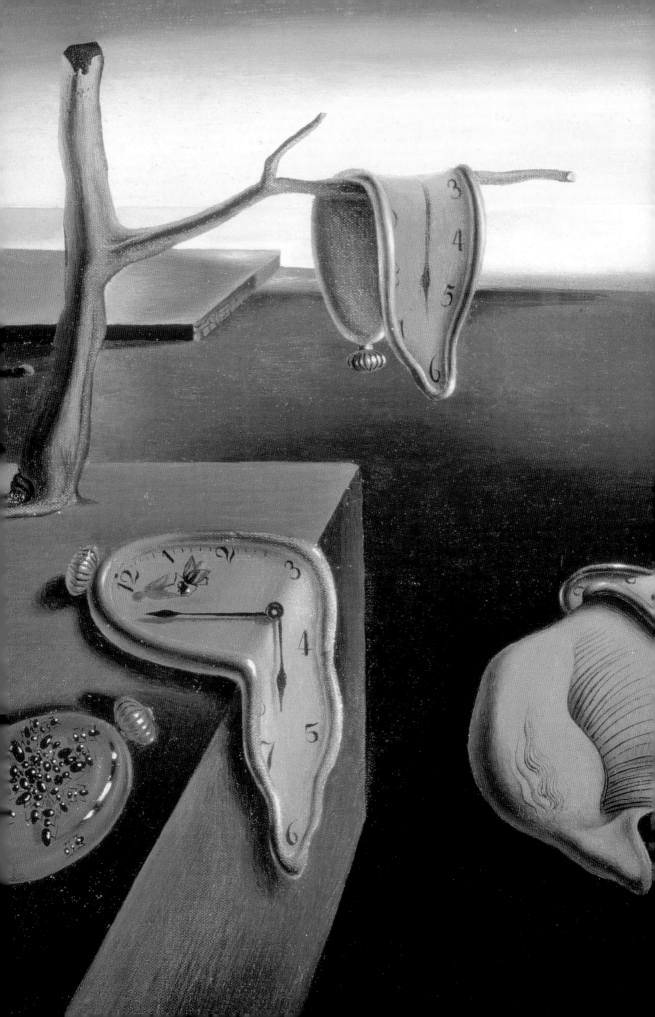

66 Collection:
an accumulation of objects
gathered for study,
comparison, or exhibition
or as a hobby. 99

Merriam-Webster's Collegiate Dictionary

It's difficult to deny that putting the words "watch" and "collection" side by side is something of a pleonasm. After all, the richness and diversity of watches are a perfect match for the dictionary definition of a collection. As for the neophyte, his or her quest always begins with the same three questions: What should I start my watch collection with? Which models should I include? Where will the collection stop? Some enthusiasts will tell you that their collections were built on the inextinguishable quest for the piece they didn't already have, and that—frustration being the driving force of 90 percent of collectors—their collections can never come to an end.

Nonetheless, most great watch accumulators started small. Though owning two watches is not enough to turn the casual enthusiast into a hardened collector, it can be considered an honest start. A collection takes shape over time and becomes better defined with each new purchase, provided each purchase follows some coherent direction, or, better yet, a concept specific to each collector. Granted, to the average man on the street, the concept behind a collection can be completely impenetrable. For instance, there was a young French collector who appeared to be a deep-sea-diving fanatic. He owned a good sixty underwater watches, but in actuality loathed water and had never been diving in his life. A psychoanalyst would probably tell you that this collection's coherence lies in the cathartic power unleashed by a hydrophobic man's purchase of underwater watches.

Whatever its contents reveal, a collection remains a matter of choice, as can be guessed from the word collection's shared Latin etymology with the word *election,* which means "to choose together." A fledgling collector's first objective is to choose the theme that will run through his future watch holdings. Initially, this will ensure that his collection doesn't become too scattered. It will also teach the collector to be discerning, by reminding him to avoid a rectangular watch, for instance, if his collection is composed of round models. As for the exact nature of a collection, there are no rules or regulations mandating that one type of collection is "good" and another "bad."

Enthusiasts often choose to collect watches that relate to another of their interests. For instance, a military man might elect to collect military watches, while an inveterate athlete might go for chronographs, and a 1930s buff might opt for "barrel" watches. Others may go so far as to collect the same model, manufactured by the same brand over different periods, without harboring any fear of monotony. Still others will push refinement to the point of exclusively collecting watches with white dials displaying silver Arabic numerals.

No matter its specialization, a collection can include both vintage pieces and new ones. Though some experts consider any model no longer in production a collector's piece, it is generally agreed that a watch is a collector's piece if its manufacturing date precedes 1980. Watches are considered secondhand if they were previously worn and are still being manufactured by brands and listed by authorized dealers. Secondhand watches are sold at auction or by specialized retailers, and are 30 to 40 percent less expensive than they would be fresh out of the factory.

The Piaget Pièce d'Or
watch encased in two
twenty-dollar coins.

Whether you decide to collect a single brand or several brands,
antique models or contemporary models, the first purchase is a crucial one. An enthusiast, and especially a novice, will have to consider three important guidelines before he succumbs to the
timepiece of his desire. First of all, he must follow his instincts—
the only good purchase is the purchase of something we truly
desire. Second, he must let himself be guided by his taste, a mys-
terious intangible that cannot be questioned. And third, he must
evaluate his financial resources. Collecting time can be extremely
expensive. A decision to purchase exclusively complicated

FOLLOWING PAGES, LEFT AND CENTER: Hunter-cased fob watch with double face. Perpetual calendar and moon
phase on back; hours, minutes, and small seconds at six o'clock on front, 1895.
RIGHT: Vacheron Constantin Chinese watch. Gold enamel watch decorated with two birds on a floral background surrounded by a line of half pearls. Duplex escapement. Geneva, 1846.

watches must be backed by a well-stocked bank account. Keep in mind that the entrance fee to the world of timepiece heavyweights manufactured over a period of years (at a cost of several million dollars) is a hefty one. You'll need $35,000 to $60,000 to enjoy the rotation of a Swiss tourbillon; $90,000 to $420,000 to set off the chimes of a minute repeater; and $12,000 to $90,000 for a perpetual calendar watch that will keep track of the date until 2100. Prices rise even higher for models with multiple functions: a triple complication watch with a minute repeater, a perpetual calendar, and a chronograph can easily cost over half a million dollars. Any watch produced in a numbered, limited edition will be considerably more valuable if the model was produced in a small run (ten rather than ten thousand), has a particular appeal from a technical point of view, is made by a preeminent name in watchmaking, or has only been released in one market. If you've managed to get the first or last number in the series, the model in question will be 30 percent more valuable on the auction block. As for unique pieces made by the great Swiss manufacturers, they can reach astronomical prices far above a million dollars. In other words, specializing in complicated watches means embarking on a journey with your bank account.

Single-brand collections are similar, in that they always imply greater expense than collections culled from the output of a variety of companies. This is particularly true if you happen to fall in love with one of the great names of Swiss watchmaking, such as Patek Philippe, which has been manufacturing some of the most beautiful timepieces in the world since 1839. Not only does this company "collect" record-breakers at watch auctions, but its most "afford-able" models start at between $10,500 and $13,000, the price that a Patek Philippe amateur will pay to acquire a simple piece such as a Calatrava, a mechanical caliber limited to displaying hours, minutes, and seconds. If you consider ten watches to be the bare minimum to constitute the beginnings of a collection, the math is simple but forbidding: plan on spending at least $60,000 for a small collection of "basic" Patek Philippe watches. And if you turn to slightly more complicated models, the prices skyrocket. For instance, a gold chronograph from the 1940s or 1950s with a mechanical movement and a leather wristband is worth $60,000 alone.

Vacheron Constantin is another prestigious watch manufacturer whose models are avidly sought by luxury watch lovers. The Geneva company, which celebrated its 250th anniversary in 2005, has seen the quoted value of some of its models rapidly double, triple, or even quadruple. A particularly notable example of this phenomenon occurred in April 2005 in Geneva, when the Tour de l'île complicated watch was sold at auction for $1.46 million, breaking all records for contemporary wristwatch sales. Vacheron Constantin watches have performed so well at auction that they are now right up there with Patek Philippe, especially when it comes to certain 1940s pieces such as the Vacheron chronographs with two counters. Nonetheless, certain ultrathin gold models launched in the 1960s remain relatively accessible at $2,500 to $6,500.

Breguet is another blue-chip company. Though the prices paid for the oldest models by the genius who invented the tourbillon reach daunting heights at auction (such as the nineteenth-century pocket watch, model number 1188, with a tourbillon, which sold for over $1.5 million in 2002), other Breguet models, such as the 1950 Type XX steel chronograph, which can be acquired for about $10,500 to $13,000, remain more reasonable. Audemars Piguet also offers extremely high-quality pieces that tend to be good investments, including a 1940s mechanical chronograph with two gold counters, generally available for around $33,000 to $40,000. Though they are now highly desirable, Jaeger-LeCoultre watches were long undervalued. Aside from the famous Reverso models, one could also invest in certain 1950s pieces, particularly Memovox automatic gold alarm watches, in its basic version, currently listed at about $2,500 to $4,000.

Rolex is another leading brand whose watches belong in the best collections. Pre-1970 mechanical versions of Rolex's most legendary model, the Daytona, reach astronomical prices, particularly the Daytona Paul Newman, which can easily exceed the $60,000 mark at auction. When it comes to this essential timepiece, even a simple dial, sold separately, can hit outrageous prices. In 2004, for instance, Sotheby's in Geneva auctioned a Daytona Paul Newman dial for $33,970. However, the basic Daytona is more affordable, its price being around $10,500. And the steel Oyster that shows only the date and was produced in the 1960s and '70s, is valued between $2,000 and $2,500. But the atypical models with moon phases and perpetual calendars (references 8171 and 6062) made by Rolex in the fifties remain extremely rare. These collector pieces begin at more than $130,000. In an entirely different style,

Chrono 130 by Patek Philippe, circa 1940.

ABOVE: Christie's London auction room.
RIGHT: The Tour de l'Ile, released by Vacheron Constantin in 2005 to celebrate its 250th anniversary. Featuring sixteen complications displayed on two faces, it is the most complicated wristwatch ever made.

the elegance of Cartier watches draws quite a few watch lovers to pieces such as the 1930s Tank models, which are currently appraised at about $18,000.

Nonetheless, a thrifty beginning collector should not despair. It is entirely possible to start a collection without ruining oneself, by buying interesting pieces produced by brands less famous than those discussed above. With a starting budget somewhere between $6,000 and $12,000, savvy beginners can explore brand names less valued by the auctioneers, such as Panerai, IWC (pro-

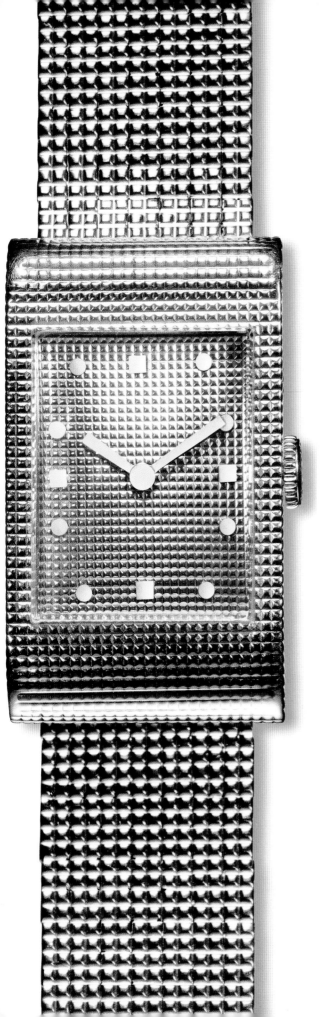

ducers of the old Portuguese models), or Omega. The latter company's models made between 1950 and 1970 are particularly interesting. A gold Constellation chronometer with center hands can be acquired for $3,500 to $4,800, while a steel Speedmaster chronometer from the 1970s won't cost you more than $1,800 to $2,500. Other choice outsiders include Longines, whose rectangular and curvex gold pieces from the 1930s are assessed at no more than $1,200, and Movado, whose gold, round watches from the 1950s are in the same price range. Also, don't overlook Universal Genève and its $4,800 Tricompax chronographs with three counters, or Breitling and its 1970s Navitimers, worth around $1,500.

Once you've set the foundations of your future collection, you'll have to build it up. In order to uncover rare finds, it is strongly suggested

Boucheron Rectangle watch, circa 1960.

that you do some research by reading specialized books and periodicals (*Montres Magazine, Europa Star, la Revue des Montres,* etc.), by consulting relevant Web sites (www.lacotedesmontres.com, www.worldtempus.com, and www.thepurists.com), and by buying auction catalogs. It takes little more than a phone call or a letter to organize delivery of Antiquorum, Christie's, Sotheby's, Bonhams, and Drouot's catalogs, but keep in mind that with leading auction houses holding about fifty international watch auctions per year, it will cost you about $1,200 just to receive all the catalogs. Another judicious choice is to consult an expert to determine the actual value of any piece you wish to acquire. Only an expert can open up a watch and see "what makes it tick." The simplest way to have a watch that you've spotted in a shop or been offered by a third

Dunhill Facet watch, circa 2000.

PREVIOUS PAGES:
(left) Brazilian aviator Alberto Santos-Dumont in March 1907, on board the No. 15 powered by an Antoinette motor.
(right) The Cartier Santos watch, 1914. Satin gold case, square bezel in polished gold, and featuring a dial signed by Cartier.

OPPOSITE: Antiquorum catalog for watch auction held in Hong Kong on July 9, 2005.

party assessed is to contact the UFE (Union Française des Experts, or French Union of Experts; tel: 01 48 01 03 17). An assessment costs 3 percent of the value of the watch that is being assessed. However, experts' services are offered free of charge during the display of lots to be sold at auction, providing an ideal opportunity to determine the quality of the pieces on sale, as well as a chance to admire the goods and try them on for size.

There is no shortage of places to acquire your collection's future treasures. The most exceptional pieces are generally sold at international auctions administered by Antiquorum, Christie's, Sotheby's, and Bonhams. More affordable pieces can be found at the Drouot auction house in Paris. Specialty stores (see the address book) are essential destinations. Both the expert advice and the variety of models offered by specialty stores are priceless tools to help the neophyte separate the wheat from the chaff.

As for Internet purchases, they are best avoided. The Internet is a vast, chaotic mix of everything from the sublime to the ridiculous, with a particular emphasis on fake Rolexes. You could potentially consider looking at watches auctioned on eBay (www.ebay.com), but again, proceed with caution: you must always be able to see the watch, try it out, and request a certificate of origin before you make a purchase.

FROM LEFT TO RIGHT:
Sean Connery playing James Bond in *Doctor No* (1962), directed by Terence Young;
American astronaut Edwin "Buzz" Aldrin posing for Neil Armstrong
during the Apollo 11 mission in July 1969. Aldrin is wearing an Omega Speedmaster Professional;
Actor's Studio portrait of Paul Newman taken during the 1950s;
Robert Redford in *Sneakers* (1993), directed by Phil Alden Robinson.

The seven most expensive watches in the world:

- **$11,002,500**:

the Henry Graves by Patek Philippe. A pocket watch with twenty-four complications. The crafting of this special commission by Henry Graves, Jr., a rich New York financier, was begun in 1928 and finished in 1933. It was sold at auction by Sotheby's New York during the Time Museum Collection sale in December 1999.

- **6,603,500 Swiss francs ($5,158,420)** :

Patek Philippe 1415 HU. A platinum wristwatch with global time. This 1946 model, which is probably unique, displays the names of forty-one cities, regions, and countries on its turning bezel. Currently the international record holder for wristwatch prices. Sold at auction in Geneva by Antiquorum in April 2002.

- **6,603,500 Swiss francs ($5,158,420)** :

Patek Philippe Caliber 89. The most complicated watch in the world. Made of white gold, it includes thirty-three complications. Conceived to celebrate the brand's 150th anniversary, the watch required nine years of development; Patek Philippe only manufactured four of them. Sold at auction in Geneva by Antiquorum in April 2004.

• **4,950,000 Swiss francs ($3,866,765)** :

yellow gold version of the Patek Philippe Caliber 89 (also with thirty-three complications). For many years, this pocket watch was the most expensive watch in the world. Sold at auction in Geneva by Antiquorum in April 1989.

• **4,137,000 Swiss francs ($3,577,279)** :

Patek Philippe reference 1526. This 1949 piece with perpetual calendar and moon phase holds a worldwide record: it is the most expensive steel wristwatch in the world, even auctionned. Sold at auction in Geneva by Christie's in April 2008.

• **3,306,250 Swiss francs ($2,582,725)** :

Vacheron Constantin King Fouad watch. The construction of this unique pocket watch began in 1914 and was completed in 1929. It features several complications (minute repeater, perpetual calendar, moon phases, and age, etc.). Sold at auction in Geneva by Antiquorum in April 2005.

• **3,207,400 Swiss francs ($2,773,372)** :

Patek Philippe reference 2497. Made in 1954, this platinum wristwatch with perpetual calendar and moon phases obtained a worldwide record for the model. It was auctioned by Christie's, in Geneva, in May 2008.

The seven commandments of the future collector:

1. You will only purchase secondhand or collectible watches from specialized dealers and/or well-established auction houses.

2. You will pay close attention to the watch's state of conservation: the case and dial must be immaculate; the hands must not be bent; the movement must work. To obtain an optimal resale price, the caliber must be signed.

3. You will require that auction houses provide you with the condition report for the piece you've acquired. The condition report is the watch's pedigree, which, in principle, guarantees its authenticity and details the various repairs and part replacements it has been subjected to over the years. This will spare you the horrors of owning a Frankenwatch: a watch whose movement and case were not made by the same watch manufacturer.

4. You will consult documents from the archives of the brand responsible for the object of your desire. These will fill you in on the watch's history, its original characteristics, and its manufacturing date. For contemporary watches, you will place your confidence only in dealers accredited by the brand.

5. You will be particularly cautious when you're interested in a watch issued in a limited run, intended, as the name indicates, never to be reissued. Certain watchmakers use a limited edition as bait for collectors, then turn around and make the same model, with a few variations, as part of their permanent collection.

6. You will never buy a Rolex, a Cartier, or any other model made by a leading brand at a street stand in Bangkok, Beijing, or Vintimille, because 99.9 times out of 100, it will be a fake. The hope of miraculously finding an authentic Rolex Oyster or a real Patek Philippe Calatrava for $100 is entirely illusory. And keep in mind that in France, for instance, the law of March 9, 2004, calls for three years in prison and a $360,000 fine for anyone found guilty of owning "merchandise presented under a counterfeit brand."

7. You will check the list of stolen fine art objects on the Art Loss Web site (www.art-loss.com) to make sure that buying the watch of your dreams will not turn you into an accessory to a crime. This is a particularly important step for those interested in buying a watch valued at over $10,000.

What accounts for the value of a collectible watch?

Until the 1970s, there were very few collectors of vintage wristwatches. Only enameled pocket watches, with and without complications, were sought out at auctions and in antique shops. Wristwatches were not even referred to as "collectible." But in 1974, Osvaldo Patrizzi opened a new market for wristwatches by founding Antiquorum, the first auction house exclusively devoted to timepieces, in Geneva.

In the mid-1980s, the revival of interest in mechanical watches, which denoted a certain social status, clearly superior to that of cheap quartz watch wearers, led to an across-the-board boom: the value of new, limited-edition watches wildly appreciated at auction, the concept of collectible watches was introduced, and the traditional Swiss watch brands were taken over by large international conglomerates. These various developments jointly contributed to a "watch phenomenon," with the result that old calibers were taken out of their workshops and attics and sold to a clientele made up of the cognoscenti.

Today the spread of auctions dedicated to timepieces has fed a field that simultaneously attracts a general audience, collectors, and a wide variety of speculators. Aside from the principle of supply and demand, it's difficult to say what determines or will determine the value of a particular piece. Experts like to state that a piece must strike a perfect balance of rarity, originality, authenticity, and aesthetic quality. More prosaically, certain surefire luxury watch brands (Patek Philippe, Vacheron Constantin, Breguet, Audemars Piguet, Lange & Söhne, etc.) rarely produce bad investments.

Auction sales can serve as valuable barometers. Nonetheless, it's important to interpret this data with the assistance of an expert, because a watch's price can sometimes shoot out of control due to a "duel" between two stubborn collectors. An expert will provide a more accurate valuation by taking into account the piece's rarity, its origin (signed case, dial, and movement), its state of conservation, and the accessories accompanying it. A watch's value can be doubled if it is sold with its original wristband, buckle, and presentation case, and of course, its documentation.

Dollar Sign, by Andy Warhol, 1982, 19.8 x 15.9 inches, Lenox Museum, New York.

The Interview

Over the past twenty years, Laurent Picciotto has watched hundreds of collectors of complicated watches in action at his Parisian shop.
Below, an interview with a man who knows exactly what makes his clients' wheels spin.

– What makes a collector?

– His collection. In other words, the act of assembling several pieces due to their beauty, their rarity, their functions, their history, and/or their price. I have a client who owns fifteen hundred watches. In his case, the theme of the collection is the number of watches he owns. Another client has only ten watches, but they are the ten most expensive watches in the world. I knew a man who collected watches and oil cans—he had eight thousand! When I asked what the relationship between these two collections was, he answered that each time he bought a timepiece or an oil can, he was retracing a history, the history of horology through watches, or the history of the automobile and aviation through oil cans.

Tic-Tac Man, portrait of Laurent Picciotto
by Anton Molnar, 1994, 25.5 x 21.2 inches, private collection.

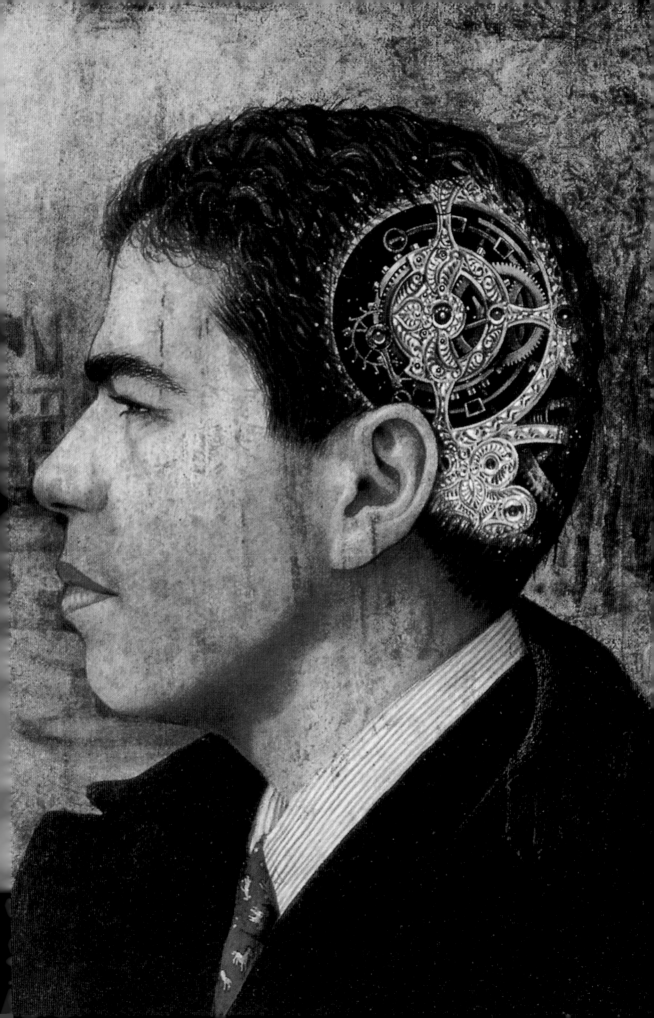

Some collectors only buy watches with black dials and Arabic numerals on white metal, no matter the brand. Others are monomaniacs obsessed with a single number, like eight, for example, and will only purchase limited–edition pieces numbered eight. A collection can also be devoted to the quest for a specific model by a single brand (such as the Audemars Piguet Royal Oak or the Rolex Daytona). Or a collector can simply get to the point where he's just filling in the blanks: he no longer really considers the watch he's buying, he's just interested in the object that will fill in the gaps in his collection—all the Breguet tourbillons, all of Patek Philippe's minute repeaters, etc. This type of collector is rare. In general, these people also tend to hoard cameras, cuff links, and cars. Their collections are like stamp albums in which not a single stamp can be missing!

– It's pathological . . .

– Yes! But the side effects are only financial. The essential characteristic of any watch collector is that he has to have a lot of money, despite the fact that none of the collectors I've met started their collections by buying $100,000 watches. Dependency comes later, as collectors acquire more pieces and their eye becomes educated. At that stage, they enter some kind of Grail quest. The watch they want to acquire is always the one they don't yet have. Frustration is the driving force of most great collectors. When a man finds himself face-to-face with a watch he has been dreaming of night and day for several months, the only reasoning he knows is: "This piece is worth $850,000. I can't really afford to buy it, but can I really resolve myself to living without it?" In 90 percent of cases, the answer is no, and he buys the watch.

– Does the act of collecting objects related to time accentuate this dependency?

– Certainly. The watch accumulator is different from the painting accumulator, for he collects the measurement of passing time. Some have the feeling they can master the flow of time by acquiring highly complex watches. Others need to fragment time by changing watches several times a day. I knew an American collector who owned more than a thousand watches; he changed watches seven times a day. Each part of his day was defined by the particular model he chose to wear: there was the shower watch, the breakfast watch, the office watch . . . And he changed all the watches from day to day. He told me he spent 25 percent of his time managing his holdings in time-measurement devices. The approach of the hour of one's death is also an integral factor of a watch collection. When some collectors get old, they sell their collections and stop wearing a watch.

- You never mention any female collectors . . .

- Because as far as I know, there aren't any. Collecting watches is typically a male activity. For men, a watch is a rite of passage. When a boy is given his first watch, he is given a "man's" accessory, an object that will help him enter the adult world. He is proud to show it off at school. A collector buying himself a new model will always glow with that same initial look of pride. I've always said that I sell expensive toys . . .

Watch Brands from A to Z

"Finally, it follows that to have a good timepiece and to avoid being fooled, one must deal directly with skillful artists." This quote—from the horology volume of Diderot and d'Alembert's *Encyclopedia*—is a fitting preamble to our A to Z of brand watches. The A to Z guide lists forty-eight companies, from A as in Audemars Piguet to Z as in Zenith. Why forty-eight rather than thirty-two, or two hundred and fifty-nine? Because the wide range of timepieces included in these forty-eight brands' collections give a fairly accurate picture of the contemporary watch market. As can be expected, the selection process was grueling. My goal was not to establish an exhaustive catalog, but to highlight companies whose models are aesthetically and/or technically interesting to the timepiece enthusiast, whether through their histories or horological accomplishments, their ability to anticipate future trends and fashions, or simply their acute sense of marketing.

This chapter spans the gamut from *haute horlogerie* manufacturers to fashion houses exclusively devoted to quartz watches, from corporations that sell over a million watches annually to independent watchmakers who produce fewer than one thousand pieces a year. The A to Z's guiding principle is the coherence of the brand, the watch, or sometimes the price. This selection is admittedly subjective, my embrace of specific approaches. It is a choice. Turn the page and discover this watch enthusiast's choice of watch brands.

All prices cited in this chapter are given as an approximate reference.

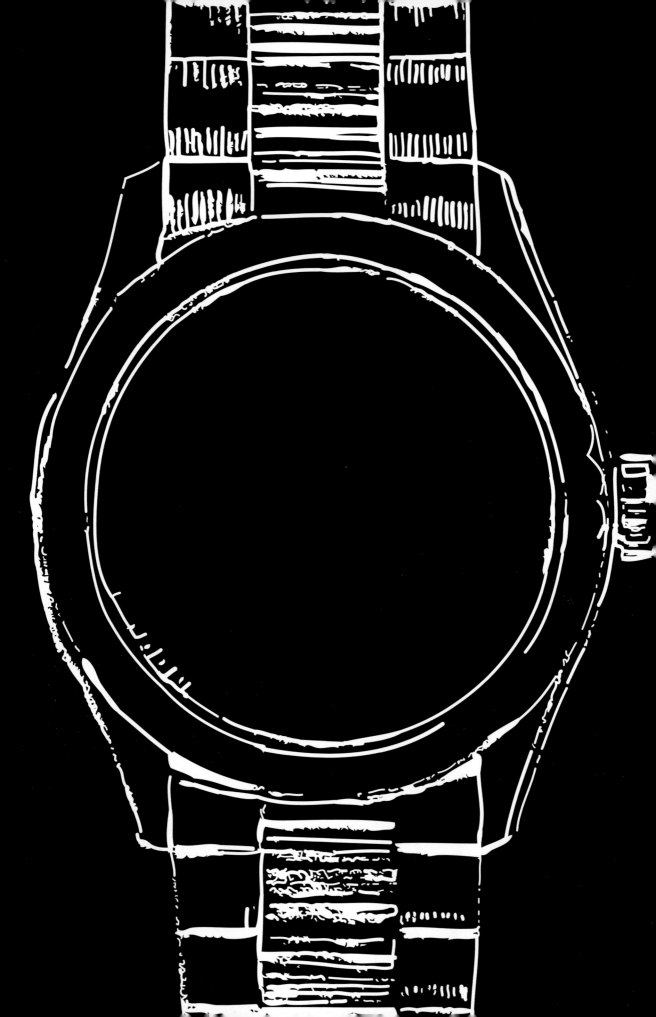

AUDEMARS PIGUET

Royal Oak Grande Complication. Perpetual calendar with moon phase, minute repeater, and split-second chronograph.

Royal Oak 3120. Automatic watch with date.

Carbon Concept Tourbillon. 30-minute linear chronograph minute counter and power reserve indicator.

SPORT WATCHES
AND CONTEMPORARY COMPLICATIONS

Ever since 1972 Audemars Piguet has been marching to the beat of one of the most famous sport watches in the world, the Royal Oak. Its other specialty, going all the way back to 1875, is in complicated movements. The timepieces born of Audemars Piguet's combination of these two different types of watches never fail to astonish.

It is always surprising when one watch, no matter how exquisitely made, eclipses all the competition. This is exactly what happened in the case of Audemars Piguet. Since the 1972 introduction of its Royal Oak, a revolutionary timepiece design by Gérald Genta, with an octagonal case and eight visible screws, collectors have forgotten that Audemars Piguet's fame was once rooted in its technical mastery of the distinguished art of watchmaking.

Founded in Le Brassus in 1875 by Jules Audemars and Edward Piguet, the company initially specialized in perpetual calendars, minute repeaters, and chronographs. It was soon trailblazing its way through the twentieth century. From the thinnest minute repeater calibers in the world to ultraflat, simple movements and automatic movements with perpetual calendars or tourbillons, from skeleton watches to unconventional "wandering hour" watches (the Star Wheel), Audemars Piguet has never failed to provide collectors with pieces to chase after. And by outfitting its best-selling sport watch with several complicated movements, the company has wisely provided Royal Oak enthusiasts with similar incentives. This decision to integrate complications into sport watches, without radically tampering with either type of timepiece's essence, has made Audemars Piguet one of the rare traditional *haute horlogerie* companies to offer a different take on complicated watches.

With an annual production of approximately twenty-eight thousand watches, the Swiss company's coherent collections are primarily based on its two strengths: classic complicated pieces (in the Jules Audemars and Edward Piguet line) and more contemporary sport (Royal Oak, Royal Oak Offshore) and urban (Millenary) models. All of Audemars Piguet's complicated calibers are either developed in-house or at the AP subsidiary by Renaud & Papi, two watchmakers once employed at the headquarters. The company used to buy movement blanks for its basic movements from Jaeger-LeCoultre but is now aiming to begin manufacturing them itself. In addition to the ultrathin 2120 automatic caliber it conceived in collaboration with Patek Philippe and Vacheron Constantin in the 1970s, Audemars Piguet developed two movements completely in-house: a mechanical movement (3090) and an automatic one (3120). The mechanisms developed by Audemars Piguet today outfit 70 percent of its models.

As for classic watches, the company is particularly well known for minute repeaters that strike in three tones. These stunning little pieces can also be fitted with a chronograph and/or a tourbillon. Here we also find very handsome skeletons, ultraflat

Jules Audemars.
Chronometer featuring new
Audemars Piguet escapement.

Jules Audemars.
Jump-hour minute repeater.

Millenary Tourbillon.
With Audemars Piguet escapement and dead seconds.

perpetual calendars, and jump hours coupled with a minute repeater.

At the same time, the company has been investing for several years in works aiming to improve the precision of the mechanical watch. In 2006, after ten years of development, it unveiled a new oil-free escapement that improves the watch's performance. The fruit of this labor first appeared in 2007 in the Millenary collection, with independent seconds, and then in 2009 in a spectacular Jules Audemars offering. Aside from the fact that this manual windup caliber boasts the highest frequency in contemporary watchmaking (43,200 alternations per hour), its construction on several levels makes one feel as though one were witnessing the creation of time itself. Audemars Piguet will only produce around twenty such pieces per year, at a price of $214,699 for white gold and $231,100 for platinum.

In the Royal Oak family, it is the Concept line that has captured the attention of the young enthusiasts. Launched in 2002, the first Royal Oak Concept, a limited series of 150 pieces designed to resemble a Formula One motor (titanium movement, shockproof tourbillon, torque gauge), quickly sold out. Less alluring in its design, the Royal Oak Carbon Concept Tourbillon and Chronograph, launched in 2008, couples a tourbillon and a chronograph in a profusion of high-tech materials (forged carbon, titanium, ceramic, aluminum), offered at a price of $226,000. Such models reflect the capacity of this brand to drive timepiece complications forward in a more contemporary manner. For instance, Audemars Piguet is the only company to offer a minute repeater that is water resistant to sixty-five feet, the Royal Oak Grande Complication ($702,000 for white gold, with a yearlong waiting list). Yet the most beautiful Royal Oak may well be its basic model, a watch that has aroused the desires of successive generations of men. Lightly altered in 2005 with the addition of a 3120 caliber, the solid-steel automatic version starts at $11,300. Fans of powerful, rugged watches will opt for another model in the same family, the Royal Oak Offshore. Issued in 1992, the Offshore is characterized by an extralarge case, high-tech materials, and particularly resistant automatic movements (antimagnetic, etc.). The chronograph is available starting at a little over $18,200. Arnold Schwarzenegger, ex-Terminator, loves it.

Those who appreciate fine watches will find that Audemars Piguet is protecting an "endangered species": the pocket watch. Indeed, this watchmaker has continued to produce the Grande Complication since 1899. It features a minute repeater, a fly-back function chronograph, and a moon phase perpetual calendar. Production time is one year, and the cost of hanging this piece of history on your vest is just shy of $1 million.

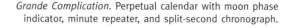

Grande Complication. Perpetual calendar with moon phase indicator, minute repeater, and split-second chronograph.

BAUME & MERCIER

CAREFREE WATCHES

Iléa.
Quartz movement.

Hampton Classic.
Automatic movement and
steel case.

Classima Executives.
Automatic chronograph with
date indicator.

This Swiss company offers a diverse range of styles at an average price of $3,100. Though Baume & Mercier's movements may not be complicated, its men's and ladies' models are consistently visually stunning. No one has ever complained about wearing a Baume & Mercier watch. Sold at a reasonable price range ($1,500 to $75,000) and in seductively simple designs.

Baume & Mercier watches are probably Richemont's most accessible brand. Baume & Mercier watches look and feel like watches, plain and simple. They are comfortable and have a good price/quality ratio, and efforts have been made to expand the mechanical watch collections. Baume & Mercier's history has included several technical benchmarks. The company was founded in Switzerland in 1830 by the Baume brothers. Between 1885 and 1893, Baume watches received three prizes for their accuracy at the Kew Observatory's chronometer competition, with, among others, a fly-back chronograph and a chronometer watch with a tourbillon. In 1920 watchmaker Paul Mercier's involvement with the company led to the creation of the Baume & Mercier brand, and most important, to its obtaining the prestigious Poinçon de Genève. By 1921 the company was already producing more pieces with the Poinçon label than any other manufacturer. Following World War II, Baume & Mercier began to offer a generalist line of watches with a particular emphasis on ladies' models. In 1950 the brand made a splash with the Marquise, the first ladies' watch to feature a rigid bracelet. In 1973 it issued the Galaxy, another ladies' watch, with an asymmetrical case that was awarded the prize for creativity at Baden Baden. Unfortunately, the company has never reissued these models.

Today Baume & Mercier has an annual output that, according to our estimates, is increasing by roughly 100,000 per year. The ladies' models account for 58 percent of Baume & Mercier's total sales, while men's models account for 42 percent. By joining the Richemont group in 1988, Baume & Mercier gained itself with an opportunity to strengthen its position in the midrange market—in fact, the CEO of the company is in the habit of describing it as one "that doesn't talk itself up, but talks directly to its customers"—and to launch new flagship collections. One of these collections, the Hampton line, launched in 1994, currently accounts for 20 percent of the company's revenues. In fifteen years, the company sold one million pieces. These rectangular city watches, redesigned in 2009, have been issued in a wide variety of more "horological" models. The basic Hampton Classic, with a steel case and an automatic movement visible from the back, is available starting at $2,490. Other models have a visible balance on the dial, a large date display, small seconds or even a power reserve

Riviera Magnum.
Automatic chronograph with
fly-back function.

Classima Executives GMT.
Automatic watch with second
time zone and power reserve.

indicator. It is a competitive line. In the same "urban" vein, the Classima Executives are well-finished round watches with a gold or steel case. In addition to the models displaying a second time zone and the power reserve, the Classima Executives automatic chronographs ($3,190) in particular are worth seeking out. Each year the company also issues more sophisticated timepieces in limited editions in the William Baume line. Of note in 2008 was a tourbillon priced at $75,000, and a mono push-button chronograph equipped with a Lajoux-Perret movement ($28,000). In 2009 enthusiasts discovered a new tourbillon housed in a gold case framing a black dial—a limited edition of ten pieces at $28,000 apiece. Though it is a little weaker in the sport watch realm, Baume & Mercier is known for its Riviera watches with dodecagonal cases that have been recrafted in a more contemporary style. Created in 1973, the Riviera line now includes enlarged automatic chronographs water-resistant to two hundred feet, which start at $3,390. The Riviera Magnum, with a steel PVD-coated chronograph with fly-back, in a limited edition of one thousand pieces is available for $7,490.

Finally, turning to ladies' watches, Baume & Mercier can pride itself on having originated the cuff-watch trend with the 1997 release of the Catwalk. The Diamant, issued in 2005, is one of its charming successors. Entirely made of steel, with a diamond on its crown, this rectangular quartz watch is marvelously graceful. As for round Baume & Mercier pieces, the Iléa is worth a look: issued in 2008, this quartz model starts at $1,990.

BELL & ROSS

PROFESSIONAL INSTRUMENTS

BR 01 Instrument.
Automatic watch with date display.

BR01 Radar.
Automatic watch with hour, minute, and second display on disks.

Airbone BR01.
Automatic watch set with diamonds.

BR01 Orange.
Diving watch with automatic movement water resistant to 3,280 feet.

Bell & Ross's unofficial motto is "We don't make watches, we make tools." The Swiss company, founded in the early 1990s by designers Bruno Belamich and Carlos Rosillo with aerospace engineer Helmut Sinn, has firmly established itself in the field of so-called professional watches. Fueled by the idea that form follows function, the trio at the head of Bell & Ross is dedicated to manufacturing efficient, reliable, and easily legible watches that meet the needs of pilots, bomb disposal experts, and professional divers.

In 1993 the company unveiled its first timepiece, the Space 1, a reissue of the first automatic chronograph developed by Sinn in 1983 and worn by the crew of the Skylab mission. In 1996 the company was commissioned by the French Emergency Response administration to develop the Type Démineur, a quartz watch with a case that is both antimagnetic and nonmagnetic. The following year, Bell & Ross released the Hydromax, whose resistance to pressure of up to 11,000 bars (36,089 feet) leaped far beyond any previous water-resistance records. Bell & Ross five lines of sophisticated watches (Professional, Classic, Vintage, Function, and Instrument BR01) are defined by the needs of the audiences they target. Every Bell & Ross watch is purely ergonomic and is manufactured to fulfill specific requirements without unnecessary embellishments. Watch hands are generally covered in tritium and set against a black dial in order to improve legibility, and models are consistently equipped with antireflective glass and tried-and-true mechanical and quartz movements (ETA, Valjoux, and Lemania). The Space 3 is a particular standout among Bell & Ross's rock-solid watches. Conceived to be worn by astronauts, it is noteworthy for a telescopic crown that retracts into the case in order to avoid being accidentally jogged and retails for $2,500. In roughly the same category, the quartz Type Démineur is available starting at $1,300, and the deep-sea quartz Hydromax can be had for $2,800. Still producing diving watches, in 2008 the brand launched the BR02, water resistant to 3,280 feet.

Attractive to the watch enthusiast is the Vintage line, inspired by military watches of the 1940s, starting at $2,000. Yet it is the Instrument BR is the watch for which Bell & Ross is especially known today. The concept for this watch is to transpose an airplane's instrument panel clock to the wearer's wrist. Launched in 2005, this truly enormous square watch (1.81 inches) now brings in more than half of the brand's sales. The line offers many models, from the BR01-93 GMT, an automatic three-hand at $4,500, to the BR Grande Minuteur tourbillon at $200,000. Among the latest offerings, worthy of mention is the BR01 Radar, a limited edition of five hundred pieces, at $4,900 each, where the hour is given by plates on a graduated dial that resembles a GPS. Also of note is the BR01 Airborne, with a case constructed around an enormous skull and crossbones, the emblem of parachutists of the U.S. Airborne Division ($5,000). At night the skull comes to life, turning a phosphorescent green—perfect for showing off at Les Caves du Roy in Saint-Tropez.

BLANCPAIN

A SENSE OF REFINEMENT

After being given new life by Jean-Claude Biver in 1982, Blancpain became a key contributor to the revival of mechanical horology in the 1990s. Today the brand continues to provide a flawlessly tasteful, contemporary take on the watchmaking complications of centuries past, with a distinct flair.

Blancpain was founded in 1735 by Jehan-Jacques de Blancpain in Villeret, Switzerland, and went on to experience many ups and downs before being bought by Jean-Claude Biver and Jacques Piguet in 1982. Until 1982 the brand was primarily known for developing one of the first automatic calibers, for Harwood, in 1926, and one of the first automatic ladies' wristwatches, the Rolls Dames, in 1930. In the absence of an heir, the Blancpain name was retired in the 1930s and the company was renamed Rayville (a phonetic anagram of Villeret). For fifty years Rayville focused on producing diving watches such as the celebrated Fifty Fathoms, launched in 1953. Then, in the early 1980s, at the peak of the quartz era, Biver and Piguet decided to revive Blancpain by returning to the brand's roots in fine mechanical horology. The company's new slogan— "Since 1735 there has never been a Blancpain quartz watch, and there never will be"— was an immediate hit. As for the watches, Biver and Piguet picked up the classic tradition of fine watchmaking right where Blancpain had left it many years earlier. In 1983 the company reinvigorated its moon phase watch with an automatic caliber (6395) that was then the smallest in the world. In 1988 the brand broke new ground with the introduction of six masterpieces of the watchmaker's art in six identical cases: the ultra-slim, the moon phase calendar, the perpetual calendar, the split-second chronograph, the tourbillon, and the minute repeater. In 1991 it introduced the 1735, which fit all the above complications in a single case. Having decisively reclaimed its credibility in the realm of complication watches, Blancpain was acquired by the Swatch Group in 1992. The company head, Marc Hayek (grandson of Nicholas Hayek), set about expanding manufacturing facilities while modernizing the design of the models.

Today the brand produces around fifteen thousand watches per year. Prices range from $7,100 for an ultrathin steel Villeret to more than $1 million for a tourbillon studded with diamond baguettes.

In addition to the movements developed based on Frédéric Piguet's, in 2006 Blancpain launched its first completely in-house manually wound caliber, the 13RO, equipped with a power reserve of eight days. Since then the manufacturer has designed a half-dozen calibers, some of which are first rate. By way of example is the Carrousel Volant Une Minute (caliber 225), introduced in 2008: this patented piece brings new attention to a horological complication invented in 1892 by the Danish watchmaker

Fifty Fathoms.
Automatic diving watch water resistant to 984 feet.

Carrousel Volant.
Carousel automatic watch that makes a complete rotation in 60 seconds.

L-Evolution Tourbillon.
Automatic movement and dual time zone.

Léman.
Alarm watch with second time zone, automatic movement, steel case.

L-Evolution.
Automatic watch with date, moon phase indicator, and 8-day power reserve.

Villeret.
Single push-button chronograph with automatic movement and white gold case.

Bahne Bonniksen, which had fallen into oblivion. Resembling a tourbillon, the carousel compensates for the effects of gravity on the movement's operation. Blancpain's feat was to miniaturize it in a wristwatch with a carousel that completes one rotation in sixty seconds. This collector's model is limited to 288 pieces (around $180,300). The brand is also known for its tourbillons that contain the mechanism conceived more than twenty years ago by the great watchmaker Vincent Calabrese. Since then Blancpain has acquired the Calabrese company and offers in its collections a dozen varieties of this prestigious timepiece complication. The brand produces two hundred such pieces per year. Among the latest offerings, of note is an automatic tourbillon in rose gold with GMT function, introduced at the 2009 Basel Watch Fair in a new line of watches named L-Evolution. This model boasts a distinctly more contemporary design (limited edition of ninety-nine pieces, $129,500 a piece). With oversize numerals, a transparency effect on the dials, counters, and redesigned functions, this line wishes to project a more modern vision of *haute horlogerie*. It offers an automatic perpetual calendar complete with an eight-day power reserve and moon phase display, and is very simple to set ($17,300).

In another domain, Blancpain is known for its chronographs such as the Villeret Chronographe Monopoussoir (single push button): released in 2004 and based on the automatic caliber 1185 (one of the slimmest in the industry), it is one of the most elegant chronographs on the market ($19,600 for white gold). The brand also offers various chronographs with fly-back function, with or without split-time counter (starting at $10,900). As for watches with more useful, day-to-day functions, one should also mention the 2003 Léman Alarm GMT, with an automatic movement, introduced in 2003, which required four years of development.

Yet Blancpain's biggest success is undoubtedly the Fifty Fathoms, which was redesigned in 2007. Perfectly proportioned in-house movements, waterproof to a thousand feet, in three years this diving watch has become this house's best-selling timepiece. The simplest model, the Fifty Fathoms Automatique, with three hands, is available for $12,800, while the most complicated, the Fifty Fathoms Tourbillon, costs $123,000.

BOUCHERON

Reflex XL.
Automatic movement with "crazy second."

Reflet XL Cruise.
Automatic watch with date display.

Automatic chronograph with date display.

Ronde Bestiaire.
Fine jewelry watch with "crazy second."

FRENCH ELEGANCE

Even Boucheron's CEO will admit that his celebrated Place Vendôme company's timepiece collections only recently emerged from a long period of creative stagnation. Yet for two years now, the jeweler (which belongs to PPR) has undergone a major overhaul: repositioning of the brand, offering more "horological" movements, and developing its jewelry watches. This house, which has practically always sold watches since its creation in 1858 in Paris, today produces between six thousand and eight thousand pieces per year. Moreover, it has a secret weapon: the famous Reflet watch, also known as a Godron watch. Created in 1948, a year after Boucheron's invention of an ingenious sliding system to effortlessly switch watch bracelets, this gadrooned and curved rectangular watch had everything required to seduce several generations of men and women. With a chic design, gold and steel models, three case sizes, an interchangeable strap allowing the wearer to assert his or her individuality, and an affordable price of $3,000 for a large in steel, the Reflet, redesigned in 2006, remains Boucheron's absolute best seller.

Launched in 2008, the XL line is interesting. Witness the Cruise, a limited edition of twenty-six pieces presented at the Basel Watch Fair in 2009. At $9,600, it comes with a steel case that opens up onto a wooden dial designed like the bridge of a Riva boat. Moreover, it is outfitted with the caliber 4000, a solid automatic movement by Girard-Perregaux, in collaboration with Boucheron since 2007. More sober, the Reflet XL Seconde Folle (Crazy Second) features a second hand that turns every sixty seconds before suddenly stopping, is run by the GP caliber 4000 and retails for $19,000 in rose gold.

Boucheron has also capitalized on its famous Godron watch by applying it to other watch lines (the Ronde and the Carrée, launched in 2005) inspired by the architecture of the Place Vendôme. The result is stylish three-hand pieces, both quartz and automatic, with date and readable chronographs, unveiled at the Basel Watch Fair in 2009. The Ronde line starts at $3,100 while the Carrée line starts at $4,600, both with a steel case and alligator strap.

Similarly, the brand is developing some models that take up the themes of its jewel collections: owl, chameleon, and serpent watches. The rich, stone-covered cases are sometimes enhanced with a *seconde folle* or a flying tourbillon. In this area Boucheron shows room for improvement.

BREGUET

A GENIUS OF THE WRISTWATCH

Since the Swatch Group acquired it in 1999, Breguet has become the Swiss watch-making giant's standard-bearer. From the tourbillon to the Marine chronograph, Breguet's collections spotlight the great inventions of Abraham-Louis Breguet, a watchmaker still considered the founding father of modern horology more than two centuries after his birth.

Everyone thought Nicolas G. Hayek was crazy when he thought of buying Breguet from its owner, InvestCorp, in the 1990s. In fact Cartier had recently turned down an offer to purchase the august timepiece company because the brand was viewed as passé. Even Hayek's colleagues in the Swatch Group wondered why he wanted "to mess around with a brand that no longer sold to anyone but the King of Morocco." Yet Hayek stuck to his guns. In September 1999 he paid an estimated 200 million Swiss francs ($151,975,700) for the company originally founded in 1755 by Paris resident and Neuchâtel native Abraham-Louis Breguet. It soon became clear that Hayek had been particularly perceptive in sensing the brand's artistic, technical, historic, and media potential. In a mere six years he put the company back on its feet. Hayek invested fifteen million Swiss francs ($11,398,200) in the Nouvelle Lemania workshops (once the suppliers of Breguet movements and certain Omega calibers) to provide Breguet with a full-fledged watch factory and renamed them Manufacture Breguet.

Next, the brand's image was reoriented to emphasize Breguet's role in the history of watchmaking. Hayek worked overtime to make it known that Breguet—watchmaker to the kings, king of the watchmakers, producer of watches once praised by Balzac, Stendhal, and Pushkin—was an integral part of Europe's cultural heritage. Hayek also pushed production of the watch that single-handedly represented Breguet's standard of excellence and would significantly expand the company's prestige among consumers: the tourbillon. By reestablishing this 1801 complication, which was invented by its founder to eliminate the effect of gravity on watch movements, as an essential component of the brand's image, Nicolas G. Hayek pulled off his gambit to boost Breguet back up the ranks of luxury *haute horlogerie* companies.

To elevate the company's prestige and add to its archive of timepieces, Hayek began traveling to auctions and buying all the Breguet masterpieces that came on the block. In 2002 he spent $1.9 million to acquire a No. 1188 tourbillon watch, circa 1808. His strategy soon paid off. Breguet is today the second-most profitable brand of the Swatch Group. Its annual sales are estimated at a half-billion Swiss francs (about $488 million), with production in the neighborhood of twenty-five thousand watches per year. What watch enthusiasts seek from Breguet is to claim a little piece of horological history for themselves. After all, from the end of the eighteenth century to the beginning of the nineteenth century, Abraham-Louis Breguet, who is considered one of the forefathers of the modern automatic watch, invented pretty much everything there was to invent in the field of timekeeping. He invented the first watches

Double Tourbillon.
Two independent tourbillons, mechanical movement, and manual winding.

Automatic watch in yellow gold with moon phase indication.

Messidor Skeleton Tourbillon.
Mechanical movement and manual winding.

Regulator Tourbillon.
Automatic movement with tourbillon, 5-day power reserve, yellow-gold case.

Type XX Chronograph.
Automatic movement with small
seconds and fly-back function,
water-resistant to 328 feet.
Steel case.

Tradition.
Mechanical watch with manual
winding.

Répétition Minutes.
Mechanical watch with manual
winding, minute repeater and
24-hour indicator.

Chronograph 5247.
Mechanical movement with manual
winding and tachymeter scale
indicator.

to be wound without a key, the "double seconds" chronometer (the forebear of the modern chronometer), the *montre à tact*, a "touch watch" that could be read by touch rather than by sight, and the *pare-chute*, which, as the first shock-absorption device for watch mechanisms, considerably improved the operation and reliability of watch movements. We also have Breguet to thank for the constant-force escapement and, of course, the Breguet Spiral. Finally, Breguet laid the foundations for modern watch aesthetics by creating guilloché dials, so-called Breguet hands and numerals (completely unadorned), and off-center hour markers.

The Breguet company's contemporary collections offer reinterpretations of the brand's rich back catalog through watches distinguished by both their dashing neoclassical appearance and their fine calibers. Today Breguet is known as the top tourbillon manufacturer in the world for the simple reason that its ten or so tourbillon models are incontestably the most beautiful and finely crafted on the market. A "simple" tourbillon with manual winding starts at $92,700; a skeletonized tourbillon, with the option to be combined with other perpetual calendar functions, costs around $130,000. In 2005, the company developed a regulator tourbillon with automatic winding and a five-day power reserve. And in 2006 a spectacular double tourbillon was developed, the first model of which, due to its complexity, was not made available until the beginning of 2009. This piece, which contains 570 components, boasts two independent tourbillons, rotating on the hour axis. As the operation of the watch corresponds to the mean rate of the two tourbillons, it is twice as accurate as a classic tourbillon and costs around $400,000. Breguet is banking on other complications, such as watches with minute repeaters that sometimes come with other functions like a perpetual calendar. Another notable Breguet model is the perpetual equation of time watch, which sells for $161,700 in rose gold. Patented in 1991, this watch displays the difference between true solar time and mean solar time, as well as serving as a perpetual calendar.

The company has also conceived a model that is particularly emblematic of the Breguet heritage: the Tradition watch. Inspired by A.-L. Breguet's "subscription watches," this model required three years of development to perfect its tribute to the founder's crucial 1790 invention: the *pare-chute*, which serves to protect the watch's balance-staff. What's most interesting about the Tradition watch is that the bridges, wheels, escapements, barrels, and other components of the movement generally hidden under the main plate are as visible as the dial. It is available in various models, one with automatic windup. It is a stunningly beautiful piece that will set you back about $32,850 in yellow gold.

Finally, Breguet is also known for two sportier lines, the Marine chronographs and the Type XX collection. In the Marine family, with a recently revamped, jazzier design, the automatic chronograph in rose gold is quite finely crafted ($28,550). The Type XX consists of automatic chronographs with fly-back functions originally designed in the 1950s for French naval aviators. With prices starting at $6,950, this is the entry-level watch for newcomers to the coveted world of Breguet.

Marie-Antoinette's Two Watches

In 1783 Abraham-Louis Breguet received an enigmatic commission from an officer in the queen's guard: to make a watch including all the complications then in existence, without any restrictions of time or cost. Breguet set to work, but the unlucky queen died before she could see the fabulous No. 160 watch, the Marie-Antoinette, which wasn't actually completed until Breguet's son brought the finishing touches in 1827. This single horological masterpiece includes a perpetual calendar, an equation of time display, a minute repeater, an independent second-hand chronograph, a power reserve, and a ther-mometer. Sadly, in April 1983 it was stolen from the Jerusalem museum to which it had been willed. Nicholas G. Hayek promised a $1 million reward to whoever found it, with no result. So the founder of the Swatch Group decided to build a replica. Between 2004 and 2008, roughly fifty watchmakers, engineers, and historians worked on the project, and a new Marie-Antoinette saw the light of day in the spring of 2008: a No. 1160 pocket watch with 823 components, all as complicated as the original. Just a few days later, the L. A. Mayer Museum of Jerusalem announced that the historic model had been found. Two watches for one queen.

The No. 1160 pocket watch, a copy of the original "Marie-Antoinette," produced in 2008.

Breguet watch No. 160, known as the "Marie-Antoinette,"
was commissioned for Queen Marie-Antoinette of France
by an officer in her guard.

BREITLING

Superocean Heritage.
Diving watch with automatic movement water resistant to 656 feet.

Bentley Mulliner Tourbillon.
Mechanical chronograph accurate to 1/6th of a second with tourbillon regulator.

Navitimer.
Automatic chronograph with circular slide rule.

In the 1980s wearing a Breitling was a clear sign of worldly success. Thirty years on, models produced by the perennial Swiss specialist in aviation watches are purchased for exactly what they are: reliable, functional, and highly professional chronographs.

When Breitling appeared on the French market in 1986, the brand was practically unknown. Only a handful of enthusiasts realized this was an august company that specialized in timepieces for pilots, and had been consistently active since Léon Breitling founded it in Switzerland in 1894. The company countered its relative obscurity with a striking advertising campaign, which soon made its reputation in France and increased its sales volume by thirty-fold. Thanks to their imposing size, wide range of gold models, and sophisticated functions, Breitling chronographs made a tremendous impression and became the status symbols of the era. Yet by the end of the 1990s the "Breitling phenomenon" was running out of steam. The company decided to improve the quality of its models by submitting every one of them for COSC chronometer certification, which guarantees a high degree of accuracy. Today Breitling is one of the rare brands able to assert that each of the 230,000 watches it produces annually is a certified chronometer. But above all, the company's current success rests on its commitment to aviation, a specialization that dates back to the beginning of the twentieth century.

Indeed, as early as 1915 Breitling was providing aviators with such flight instruments as the first wristwatch chronographs. In 1923 the brand broke new ground by developing the first independent chronograph push button—until that point the chronograph's start and return-to-zero functions had been controlled via the winding crown. In 1934 the company developed a dedicated second push button for setting the chronograph to zero. This invention, which allowed for several successive short time periods to be measured, established the chronograph's current configuration. In the 1940s Breitling became the official supplier to Britain's Royal Air Force and released the Chronomat, the first chronograph fitted with a circular slide rule for aerial navigation. The slide rule, which allows pilots to make all flight plan calculations while in the air, was further developed with the 1952 launch of the Navitimer. Boasting a veritable "navigation computer," the Navitimer quickly became a reference in aeronautic timepieces and one of Breitling's mainstays. In 1969 Breitling, which generally equipped its hand-wound models with Vénus movement blanks, collaborated with Dubois Déparaz, Hamilton-Büren, and Heuer-Léonidas to develop the Chronomatic, the first automatic chronograph movement with a microrotor.

Although the majority of Breitling's mechanical calibers are developed from ETA and Valjoux bases, the brand recently unveiled its first complete in-house movement in 2009. Five years of development were necessary to manufacture this B01, an automatic chronograph with column wheels containing 346 components, equipped with a rapid date change and a power

Emergency.
Quartz watch equipped with a distress signal microtransmitter broadcasting on the aircraft emergency frequency.

Chronomat B01.
Automatic chronograph.

Chronomatic 1461.
Automatic chronograph with perpetual calendar and moon phase indicator.

reserve of more than 70 hours. With this caliber, Breitling is entering the very small circle of Swiss manufacturers capable of manufacturing this type of piece. The company expects to produce fifty thousand of them per year. As for its quartz models, since 2001 they have been outfitted with SuperQuartz movements ten times more accurate than ordinary quartz. Breitling's watches are known for their accuracy, reliability, and durability. The Chronomat was initially reissued for the pilots of the elite Italian Frecce Tricolori flight team in 1984; this chronograph has since been altered several times. For example, the Chronomat Evolution, water resistant to one thousand feet, features a more ample case, along with the line's trademark rotating rider-tab bezel, whose movable rider tabs are used to mark times and to simplify manipulation of the bezel. The Chronomat Evolution's self-winding movement is a caliber 13 with a frequency of 28,800 vibrations per hour, the same used in other Chronomat models. Starting at $4,650, the Chronomat Evolution is one of the best-selling Swiss automatic chronographs on the market. Purists will prefer the Chronomat B01, the first model to use the manufacturer's own chronograph movement B01, available for $38,525 in rose gold.

The Navitimer, Breitling's other emblem, features the celebrated circular slide rule used to convert miles to nautical miles or kilometers, to compute the rule of three, and to calculate currency exchanges, retailing for $6,450 in steel. Aside from the basic model, the Navitimer is available with a fly-back function (Navitimer Heritage), with a dual time zone (Navitimer World), or with a moon phase (Montbrillant), with prices ranging from $5,660 to $29,350.

Breitling has also developed a highly sophisticated line of multifunction quartz watches for aviation professionals. This new line includes the Aerospace, whose digital and analog display is designed to be user friendly and easy to read, and the Emergency, which is outfitted with a distress signal microtransmitter that broadcasts on the aircraft emergency frequency. For diving enthusiasts, the Superocean Heritage 46, a reissue of a model first launched in 1957, deserves mention. Water resistant to 656 feet, this automatic watch is not lacking in style and sells for $3,765 in steel.

On an entirely different front, Breitling in 2003 entered a partnership with Bentley automobiles. The resulting Breitling for Bentley line of watches attracts a prestigious, high-end clientele. Aside from its three automatic chronographs (including a model that measures elapsed time to one-eighth of a second, one featuring a large date display, and a jump hour, the Flying B), the Breitling for Bentley line features a bold step into timepiece complications: the Breitling for Bentley Mulliner Tourbillon. The inspiration for this complication watch came from the workshop that personalizes Bentley cars in accordance with their owners' every wish, with options ranging from $153,730 for rose gold, up to $315,000. As befits such a rarefied timepiece, the Bentley Mulliner Tourbillon's caliber is truly exceptional: the tourbillon is designed by Renaud & Papi (Audemars Piguet). A curiosity.

BULGARI

A SENSE OF SCALE

The number-three company in the global jewelry business didn't really enter the timepiece market until the late 1970s. By then, of course, Bulgari had already issued the well-known Tubogas, featuring a sinuous, snakelike design, but it had never established a comprehensive, fully developed line of watches. The brand's real debut in watchmaking came in 1977 with the launch of the Bulgari-Bulgari, its first watch produced for broad distribution. Despite the prevailing trend for ultraslim watches, the Bulgari-Bulgari's thick cylindrical case and bezel, featuring the company's name repeated twice, created an immediate sensation. In fact, the Bulgari-Bulgari was so successful that by the early 1980s the company decided to open a timepiece subsidiary in Neuchâtel, Switzerland.

Timepieces now account for a quarter of the Italian group's sales. Bulgari's watch collection consists of about ten highly stylized lines. The company's watches are immediately recognizable thanks to their sculpted design, with imposing cases and predominantly curved edges typical of popular perceptions of Italian luxury goods. In other words, Bulgari watches are both powerful and elegant, and rarely go unnoticed. As far as movements go, Bulgari hedges its bets by producing both quartz and mechanical models. For several years Bulgari maintained a contract with Girard-Perregaux to provide its automatic calibers, but now generally purchases its calibers from a variety of Swiss suppliers (ETA, Frédéric Piguet, etc.).

Additionally, Bulgari's takeovers of Gérald Genta and Daniel Roth in 2000 have allowed it to move into the complication field, with such models as the 2004 Bulgari-Bulgari tourbillon developed by Daniel Roth and produced in a limited edition of twenty-five pieces. Since then the brand has released complicated pieces each year in its various lines (Assioma, Diagono, etc.). Of note among the latest is the automatic model with tourbillon and perpetual calendar with four retrograde functions (date, day, year, month), available in a new line, Sotirio Bulgari, launched in 2009 to celebrate the brand's 125th anniversary. This collector's piece, limited to thirty in number ($213,000), is rather sober in its style. In this same line, where for the first time the Bulgari logo does not appear on the bezel of the models, there is also a beautiful retrograde date display in rose gold, available for $17,400. The module was developed completely in-house. It also appears combined with a very stylish annual calendar.

The Assioma line of watches, launched in 2005, eschews square and round shapes in favor of an elegant curved form and is clearly representative of the Bulgari style. The Assioma is available in a steel case with an ETA automatic movement and

Assioma.
Automatic chronograph with date display. Yellow gold case.

Sotorino.
Automatic tourbillon watch and perpetual calendar with retrograde hands.

retails from $4,000. The slightly sportier Ergon, which has been on the market since 2004, is a beautifully ergonomic line highlighting cases that appear to be completely integrated into the strap. Certain models are further equipped with a Dubois-Déparaz movement. Small complications can be found in this line, such as the chronograph with fly-back function and simultaneous triple time zone indicator ($5,800).

Bulgari-Bulgari.
Mechanical watch with manual winding and power reserve indicator.

Diagono.
Automatic chronograph with date display.

CARTIER

THE ESSENCE OF TIME

For over a century this celebrated Place Vendôme jeweler has employed an innate sense of materials and form to produce incomparably stylish watches such as the Tank, the Santos, the Pasha, the Tortue, and the Ballon Bleu. Cartier's inventory includes landmark watches, complicated editions, and extravagant jewelry timepieces—in other words, more than enough to draw collectors and aesthetes the world over.

Few brands boast as rich and diverse a historical catalog as Cartier. This is partially due to longevity. "The jeweler to the kings and the king of the jewelers" was founded in Paris in 1847 and began making watches soon after. In 1853 Cartier released its first gusset watches, and in 1888 it unveiled the first jewelry wristwatches. Throughout this period, Cartier bought its movements from great Swiss watch manufacturers such as Vacheron Constantin and Audemars Piguet. At the turn of the century, however, Cartier broke with tradition and entered into an exclusive agreement with Edmond Jaeger, by which Jaeger committed to providing Cartier with his entire production of ultraflat, repeater, chronograph, split-time counter, calendar, and all other complicated movements. In fact, one of the defining characteristics of Cartier's history is its longstanding reliance on top-notch watchmakers to manufacture its movements. Cartier collaborated with, among others, Patek Philippe in the 1930s and Girard-Perregaux and Frédéric Piguet in the 1980s and 1990s, and it continues to hire Jaeger-LeCoultre to manufacture some of its movements (both brands now belong to the Richemont group).

Louis Cartier set the standard for his company's style of watches by concocting a blend of elegance, daring, and innovation. In 1904 he designed the Santos for Brazilian aviator Santos Dumont. Considered the first wristwatch of its era, the Santos Dumont was issued commercially in 1911. In 1906 the Tonneau watch was released with a curved band that followed the line of the wearer's wrist to perfection. In 1909 Cartier patented its system for wristbands with deployment clasps. In 1912 the Tortue and the elongated Baignoire were issued, followed in 1917 by the streamlined Tank, inspired by British tanks. In the 1930s Cartier was commissioned to design a luxury waterproof watch for the Pasha of Marrakech, which led to the creation of the celebrated Pasha line.

Following its takeover by an investment group in the 1970s, Cartier inaugurated a more quotidian take on luxury objects with the Must line. Though the brand was now heavily diversifying its output through the production of lighters, leather goods, and perfume, it continued to score big hits on the timepiece market. Among Cartier's more memorable recent successes, one cannot overlook the shapely gold-and-steel Santos, which was released in 1978 and went on to sell more than one million pieces; the Panthère, which became the must-have ladies' model of 1983; the 1985 Pasha, which heralded the trend for large calibers; the 1989 Tank Américaine; and the 1996 Tank Française.

Tank Américaine.
Flying tourbillon watch with mechanical movement and manual winding.

Ballon Bleu.
Automatic movement with date indicator.

Santos 100 Skeleton.
Mechanical movement with manual winding.

Pasha 42.
Automatic watch.

Santos Dumont.
Ultraflat mechanical movement
with manual winding.

Baignoire Grande.
Mechanical watch with manual
winding.

Doña.
Quartz watch.

Today Cartier's production is estimated at five hundred thousand pieces a year, and the company is an undeniably powerful force on every tier of the watch market. Though Cartier remains the global number one in jewelry watches thanks to a constant flow of inventive new pieces, since the late 1990s the brand has also reinforced its position in the technical realm. In 2001 the company went so far as to open a timepiece division in La Chaux-de-Fonds, Switzerland, followed a few years later by the construction of a workshop in Geneva. Though until then the company had been offering only occasional complicated pieces (minute repeaters, tourbillons, etc.), it began developing a more substantial line of *haute horlogerie* watches for its Collection Privée Cartier Paris (also known as CPCP). Beginning in 2010 or 2011, this line should account for 20 percent of Cartier's annual sales and Cartier is already the second best-selling company of tourbillon pieces in the world, after Breguet.

These sophisticated movements, some of which bear the Poinçon de Genève, are for the most part developed on bases purchased from other Richemont group brands (Jaeger-LeCoultre, Roger Dubuis, etc.). Over time, the jeweler intends to begin developing all of its calibers independently. For the moment, these in-house movements are employed in the brand's most iconic models. Their common denominator is a very identity-oriented aesthetic: guilloché dials, Roman numeral markers, sword hands. In addition to the lavish Rotonde, a sapphire skeleton tourbillon with ten days of power reserve, a unique piece at roughly $1 million, the house introduced ten complex and well-chosen models at the latest Salon de Genève—for example, a graceful Tank Américaine, equipped with a flying tourbillon ($97,600) and a movement with the Poinçon de Genève; the transparent Santos 100 Skeleton, emphasizing a distinguished and contemporary movement, or the Rotonde chronograph with central display offering ease of readability for intermediary times ($37,900). Several iconic Cartier lines are retaking the world by storm. First and foremost is the Ballon Bleu. Released in 2007, in two years this unisex piece, with a case as smooth as a pebble, has become Cartier's new block-buster, which the company offers in several versions, including a tourbillon released in 2008. The yellow-gold-and-steel model starts at $6,900. Next is the Santos line, with two new models launched on its centenary in 2004. Well crafted despite its large dimensions, the automatic Santos 100 is a sporty, distinguished piece and is water resistant to 330 feet ($7,000 for the stainless steel model). The ultraflat model with a manual windup caliber, the Santos Dumont, is doubtless one of the most elegant luxury watches on the market ($13,400 in rose gold).

Another best seller is the Pasha, revisited in 2005. Now featuring a flatter, larger case (1.65 inches), the new Pasha 42 contains the automatic Caliber 8000MC, designed in collaboration with Jaeger-LeCoultre ($11,300 in steel). Finally, in 2006 the jeweler launched the Doña for women, with a unique case attached to an alligator strap that is rich in character ($7,750 for the small model). In 2009 Cartier also revamped its famous Baignoire ($8,100 in rose gold). With a jazzier design and cleaner, crisper lines, it attractively embodies the Cartier spirit.

CHANEL

FULL-TIME ICON

Launched in 2000, the J12 now represents Chanel's best-selling timepiece. Its worldwide success is a harbinger of a new style of sleek, unisex, and high-tech watches.

The success of the J12, the first ceramic sport watch by Chanel, was initially predicted by none other than . . . Rolex! At the Basel Watch Fair, Chanel's then artistic director, Jacques Helleu, a J12 prototype on his wrist, ran into one of the executives in charge of the number-one luxury watch, who told him: "You should put that in the stores right away. That watch is going to be a big success." The Rolex exec knew what he was talking about: in barely ten years, the J12 has become Chanel's top seller by a long stretch, to the point that it has eclipsed Chanel's other timepieces and has joined Chanel No. 5 perfume as one of the company's icons. Though Chanel Horlogerie does not divulge its sales volume, we do know that the J12 today accounts for more than three-quarters of its sales.

Creating this winner was far from an easy task, however. The J12 would never have seen the light of day without the insistence of its stubborn mastermind, Jacques Helleu, who passed away in 2007. He persisted at a time when nobody saw any use in Chanel entering the men's watch market, especially with a sport watch. At the time, after all, Chanel's target audience was women. Chanel first entered the watch market in 1987 with the Première, now the company's second-strongest seller. Chanel soon asserted its legitimacy in the business by buying its supplier's workshops in La Chaux-de-Fonds, Switzerland, in 1993.

Originally Chanel's watch collections were all based on iconic Chanel symbols: the Première was inspired by the No. 5 flask; the Camélia, by Coco Chanel's favorite flower. There was also the Matelassée and the Chocolat, borrowing from the emblematic design of the company's handbags, and the Mademoiselle, celebrating Gabrielle Chanel's pearls. The inspiration for the J12, however, was drawn from Jacques Helleu's interest in automobiles and sailing. "I initially created the J12 for myself, because I couldn't find a single men's watch that was entirely black, but of a brilliant, inalterable, and timeless black," Helleu explained. The company embarked on a quest for the ideal material that would be resistant to light, heat, and shock. Black ceramic, which is used in aeronautics to make certain brake discs, caught the artistic director's eye. Yet with the exception of Rado (Swatch Group), which uses ceramic as its signature material, and IWC, which made an attempt twenty years ago with the Da Vinci in white, nobody in the timepiece business was taking a chance on this material. To make matters more complicated, Helleu wanted his watch to be round, considered impossible with ceramic. Seven years later a solution finally arrived from Japan: the ceramic would not be machined but molded, allowing for a round case and curved links that hug the shape of the wearer's wrist. Named J12 after a racing sailboat, this beautiful

J12.
Tourbillon watch with a ceramic plate. Limited edition of 12 pieces.

Mini Première.
Ladies' quartz watch with diamond-set bezel.

J12.
Automatic watch in black ceramic.

J12.
Ceramic watch with automatic
caliber 3125 developed by
Audemars Piguet.

J12 Noir Intense.
Automatic watch with baguette
pavé in black ceramic.

automatic watch molded of luminous ceramic immediately met with overwhelming success. The initial run sold out within a few months, and production still appears to be inferior to demand.

Next, Chanel decided to expand its collection with another strategic move forward into the sport-watch market. In 2002 a chronograph version of the J12, water resistant to 650 feet, was launched. This new opus's automatic movement was certified as a chronometer by the COSC. At $6,800, it is still flying off the shelves. The masterstroke came in 2003 when the company switched the color of the J12 from black to white. Introduced at the Basel Watch Fair, where Chanel was exhibiting for the very first time, the white ceramic J12 was a hit among industry insiders, who were surprised by the cohesion of the watch's technical aspects and its style, and with the general public, which was bewitched by the white magic radiating from this opalescent ceramic creation. Whether the celebrity wrist it is decorating is David Beckham's or Eminem's, Caroline of Monaco's or Kylie Minogue's, the white J12 has proven that it suits all types. The quartz model starts at approximately $4,500 for the automatic pieces.

In 2004 Chanel released a chronograph version of the white J12 and a particularly luxurious limited-edition collection. Made of white or black ceramic, the J12 is now part of annual special editions produced in very limited quantities. They sell for a fortune (some up to a half-million dollars) and have found their market in Russia, Asia, and the Middle East. Though these precious-stone models were not particularly noteworthy from a horological point of view, Chanel did break new ground in 2005 by launching a J12 with a tourbillon: for the first time the plate serving as a base for the movement was made of high-tech ceramic. This was impressive, as the J12's style was not compromised by the addition of the complication, and Abraham-Louis Breguet's tourbillon has retained its indomitable spirit of technical achievement. In 2008, in the same quest for sophistication in its timepieces, Chanel released the J12 caliber 3125, with an automatic movement developed with Audemars Piguet. With a gold-and-ceramic case on leather, this J12 timepiece starts at $25,000. In 2009 one again encounters the caliber 3125 in a quite spectacular model limited to five pieces, the J12 Noir Intense, entirely studded with baguettes in ceramic black, at a price just as extraordinary as the piece: $312,000.

Finally, Chanel continues to capitalize on its ceramic empire by introducing such pieces into the Première line as an extremely feminine miniwatch with a ceramic case set on a thin rubber strap. The price of high fashion: $3,850.

CHOPARD

Chopard has long been famous for its strikingly fanciful watches for women, the Happy Diamonds. But that wasn't enough. In 1996 the company set out to conquer the men's watch market by creating its own watch manufacture in Switzerland. Chopard's efforts did not disappoint: the calibers produced in Fleurier have consistently been of the highest quality.

Chopard, official sponsor of the Cannes Film Festival. Chopard, friend to royalty and to the stars. Chopard, the company that never misses an opportunity to raise funds for charitable causes, from AIDS research to hunger relief in Africa: it's hard to miss this highly media-savvy brand. Though Chopard has been known to annoy more than a few people, one cannot fault it for bringing a breath of fantasy and bonhomie into the overly serious timepiece business.

The story begins in 1963, when two German jewelers, Karl and Karin Scheufele, took over the Chopard watchmaking company, founded in 1860 by Louis Ulysse Chopard. In less than thirty years the couple turned the little Swiss company into a world-famous brand. The key to the new Chopard's success was a model created in 1976 by Ronald Kurowski, then a designer for the company. Kurowski dreamed up a watch with diamonds moving freely between the dial and the glass, creating a virtual shower of gems. Soon the first Happy Diamonds had seen the light of day. At the slightest movement of this very era-specific watch, the thirty diamonds in its double-tonneau case were whipped into a dance against its onyx dial. Back in the 1970s, when elegant men weren't above wearing a diamond watch, the Happy Diamonds was targeted at men. Today, however, the Happy Diamonds has forsaken men for women. With hundreds of models of Happy Diamonds watches and, since 1979, jewelry pieces exclusively for women, Chopard has turned its concept into a global sensation that brings in a significant portion of its sales, ranging in price from about $6,000 to $45,000. Numerous variations on the basic theme of this classic quartz movement are issued annually (Happy Sport, Happy Spirit, etc.).

Chopard's next strategic move was to break into the exclusive club of traditional luxury timepieces. Aside from the Mille Miglia collection (chronographs annually released in the colors of the automobile race of the same name), Chopard's collections for men long lacked a cohesive feeling, both in style and in components, which were purchased from ETA, Jaeger-LeCoultre, or Frédéric Piguet. In 1996 the company decided to open the workshop in Fleurier to create its own movements. Following four years of development and an investment of some $3 million, Chopard revealed its first opus: the L.U.C 1.96 caliber, an automatic movement with a double barrel and a power reserve of more than

L.U.C Quattro Regulator.
Hand-wound mechanical watch with "regulator" display, second time zone, and 9-day power reserve.

Happy Diamonds.
Quartz chronograph with moving diamonds on dial.

Mille Miglia.
Automatic chronograph with date indicator.

L.U.C Lunar Big Date.
Automatic watch with large
date display and moon phase
indicator.

L.U.C Chrono One.
Automatic chronograph with
fly-back function.

L.U.C Tourbillon Tech Twist.
Mechanical watch with manual
winding, tourbillon, and silicium
escapement.

seventy-five hours. Recognition was quick, and the L.U.C 1.96 was chosen as Switzerland's 1997 Watch of the Year (from $16,400). In 2000 Chopard released its first manually wound mechanical movement, the L.U.C Quattro, which was fitted with four barrels and a nine-day power reserve ($30,130). The next year Chopard struck again with the L.U.C Tonneau, the first watch in the world to have a shaped automatic movement with a microrotor ($21,670 in white gold).

To date Chopard's workshop has developed a half-dozen house calibers, the vast majority of which are certified as chronometers by the COSC. Among its most notable models is the elegant Quattro Régulateur, whose "regulator" display (the minute hand is separate from the hour hand) also has a time zone and calendar aperture ($38,840 in yellow gold). The L.U.C Lunar One watch, launched in 2005, has an automatic perpetual calendar with an orbital moon phase display that only varies by one day every 122 years. In 2009 the Lunar appeared in a simplified model with large date display and small seconds in a limited edition of five hundred pieces ($57,000 in rose gold). Also well regarded, the L.U.C Chrono One, the first in-house chronograph, launched in 2006, is an automatic caliber with column wheels and boasts a fly-back function ($37,650 in rose gold). Chopard has also produced the L.U.C Tourbillon, a half-skeleton tourbillon with four barrels ($147,000). It is one of the rare tourbillons on the market to have a nine-day power reserve and to be certified by the COSC. The brand is also offering a limited series of a new silicon escapement tourbillon (the Tech Twist, about $160,000)—a prelude to the development of a new high-frequency caliber. Indeed, Chopard is in the process of working on a high-frequency mechanism (between eight and ten hertz) that should see the light of day sometime in 2010 or 2011. Its purpose is to improve the accuracy of the mechanical watch and to offer better timing. In a more basic vein, the ultraflat L.U.C XP is a classic: its simplicity is equaled only by the excellence of its movement ($11,700).

Though the workshop's watches have established their pedigree as luxury time-pieces—Chopard has even joined forces with four other companies to launch a new label, Qualité Fleurier, with extremely refined aesthetic and technical criteria—they continue to be manufactured at a particularly slow rate, with only between four thousand and five thousand L.U.C watches released annually. This represents but a small percentage of Chopard's total production, which, including all models of the company's collections, currently expands at a rate of seventy new models per year.

CORUM

THE CRAFT OF SINGULARITY

This Swiss brand's collections contain a stunningly eclectic range of watches, taking in everything from transparent tourbillons and baguette movements to regatta chronographs and coin watches. Corum is a curiosity cabinet well worth digging into.

Corum was founded in 1955 in La Chaux-de-Fonds, the birthplace of Swiss horology, by watchmaker Gaston Ries and his nephew René Bannwart, who had trained at Patek Philippe and Omega. What started out as another by-the-books Swiss watchmaking story quickly evolved as the duo created delightfully forward-looking watches and developed a reputation for being "timepiece trendsetters." For instance, when the company hadn't delivered enough dials to be ready for the 1958 Basel Watch Fair, the duo replaced the missing dials with plain gold plates—spontaneously inventing watches without hour markers on the dial. Six years later, Corum had a hit by riding the coin-watch trend with the American Double Eagle, a model with a dial made of a $20 gold coin. In the 1980s, the company released two radically different models: the Admiral's Cup, a sport watch intended as a tribute to the race of the same name; and the Golden Bridge, an innovative timepiece whose miniature baguette movement, vertically suspended in a transparent case, was designed by Vincent Calabrese.

Though Corum's mix of eclecticism and horological audacity had fallen out of public favor by the dawn of the twenty-first century, the company managed to seduce a leading figure in high-fashion watches, Severin Wunderman, the founder of Gucci Timepieces (who passed away in 2008). In 2000 Wunderman sold his company to PPR and bought Corum, which had barely been keeping its head above water by producing a mere nine thousand pieces a year. He helped the company rise from its ashes, particularly with the introduction of the Bubble, a unique watch with a glass design resembling a magnifying glass that looks as though it came straight out of a comic strip. The Bubble was a hit between 2000 and 2005: Corum sold more than eighty thousand.

In 2006, the watchmaker changed strategy: it phased out the Bubble and decided to refocus its attention on its basic lines (Admiral's Cup, Golden Bridge, Romvlvs). Today, with production of eighty thousand watches per year, Corum is highlighting one of its mainstays, the Admiral's Cup line. These watches, with nautical pennants that serve as hour markers, have been completely redesigned. With bolder lines, larger cases, and high-tech materials (titanium, carbon fibers), the Admiral's Cup symbolizes to perfection the image Swiss watchmakers are forging for the sport watch of the twenty-first century: powerful and virile. Here we find simple chronographs with split-time counters, as well as models that display two different time zones and calculate the tidal coefficient (the Tides 48): there's even an unlikely model in rose gold with a tourbillon.

Ti-Bridge.
Mechanical watch with manual winding and linear movement.

Admiral's Cup Tides 48.
Automatic watch with tide coefficients.

Coin Watch.
Watch with automatic movement hidden within a gold coin.

Golden Bridge Lady.
Mechanical watch with manual winding and linear movement.

Another flagship line is the Golden Bridge, with a wide variety of offerings. The most contemporary, the Ti-Bridge, was unveiled at the 2009 Basel Watch Fair. It runs on the caliber Co-007, the second movement to be developed completely in-house. This linear movement thus reestablishes its "bite" through the use of titanium components, a more distinguished line, and an extended power reserve of three days. This limited production of less than a thousand pieces per year is priced in the neighborhood of $12,009.

In a completely different vein, Corum has succeeded in attracting fans of curious timepieces with its skeleton tourbillons. With its main plate and bridges carved of sapphire glass, the Classical Billionaire Tourbillon set with sapphires and diamonds conveys an impression of stunning purity ($372,000). Corum is also known for having revived craft techniques that had fallen into disuse, such as miniature painting and stone marquetry.

Corum watches like the Buckingham can be excessively kitsch or extraordinarily well made, depending on the year.

DIOR

Chiffre Rouge.
Automatic chronograph developed by Hedi Slimane for Dior Homme. Steel case and bracelet.

Christal.
Quartz watch with "diamond-point"-cut sapphire glass bracelet.

Mini D de Dior.
Quartz watch with diamond-set bezel.

AND DIOR CREATED THE LADIES' WATCH...

A legendary fashion designer, the sophistication of its watches, a Swiss label. The timepiece collections of the august Parisian company headquartered on Avenue Montaigne are just like its ready-to-wear lines: always on target and seriously effective.

According to a consultant in luxury products, "Dior's success rests on an interesting paradox: the older the brand gets, the younger, and wider, its audience becomes." The meteoric rise of Dior watches, which now account for a significant portion of the company's total sales figure, is certainly eloquent testimony to this unusual dynamic.

The first timepiece branded Dior was introduced in 1975. Named the Bagheera, it was produced under license by Benedom and drew a clientele predominantly of women in their fifties. Thirty years later the Malice, the brand's best seller, launched in 2001, is largely favored by women under thirty. In other words, over the course of a few decades, Dior has cut the average age of its customer base by half.

In 1995 John Galliano's appointment as chief designer for Dior's haute couture and ready-to-wear divisions led to a general refocusing of the brand and an overhaul of its timepiece collections. Four years later LVMH took over its licensee Benedom and set up a division eligible for the Swiss Made label, the idea being to create a collection of watches that reflected the new Dior look imagined by Galliano. Once Dior's timepiece division was established, the darling of the fashion pages supervised the conception of every model. Every watch is branded with his unmistakably eclectic, offbeat, sexy, and audacious touch. By applying these values to all its products, Dior defined a desirable and more accessible take on luxury, but especially succeeded in transforming its timepieces into a natural extension of its fashions. In 2000 and 2001 the brand set the foundations for its timepiece collection by launching four lines (Malice, Diorific, Riva, and Chris 47), each of which represented a different facet of the new Dior woman.

The fashion-watch synergy was a roaring success, on a par with that experienced by Chanel with its famous ceramic J12. On the other hand, by this time an increasing number of fashion watches and new brands had muddied the water, dragging down the market. Dior attempted to rectify the situation by not putting all its eggs in the watch-as-fashion-accessory basket; the change in direction toward more "horological" collections was emerging. The company had already taken an initial step toward more timeless pieces with the 2003 launch of the D de Dior, reminiscent of certain 1960s Piaget models. Designed by Victoire de Castellane, the head of Dior Joaillerie, D de Dior is characterized by round cases, dials made of colorful precious stones and gold, and prices ranging from $1,900 to upwards of $20,000. The latest creation, launched in 2009, is the Baby Dior, an elegant, diminutive timepiece and the most well made.

Christal.
Ghost hands and quartz
movement hidden in bezel.

Christal Tourbillon.
Set with diamonds and rubies.

The second act came in 2004, when Hedi Slimane, then chief designer for Dior's men's ready-to-wear, released the Chiffre Rouge, the first Dior model with an automatic movement. This watch targeted urban professionals in their thirties with a taste for fine timepieces, as is evident from the limited series of chronographs equipped with the famous caliber El Primero by Zenith (also an LVMH company) and models displaying a second time zone ($3,600). Indeed, among contemporary sport watches, the Chiffre Rouge has no reason to be ashamed: these models are stylish and remain relatively affordable ($2,100 for the simple automatic movement). The latest move in Dior's strategy to emphasize luxury is the Dior Christal, specially designed by John Galliano. This glam-rock wonder, released in September 2005, boasts bracelets and bezels covered in "diamond point" sapphire glass. In less than five years Dior has made it the cornerstone of its timepiece offerings by increasing the number of models (still mostly quartz), case sizes, stones (diamonds, rubies, amethysts, etc.) and the prices—now averaging from $1,900 to more than $2,500. After launching the first Christal with tourbillon in 2008, Dior in 2009 unveiled a second, studded with diamonds and rubies, for the modest sum of $1.3 million. More innovative is the Christal with mysterious hours, with a quartz movement that is hidden beneath the bezel in the periphery of a transparent dial composed of transparent sapphire disks—a truly original piece that was released at the end of 2009, with a price in the neighborhood of $30,000.

EBEL

After changing hands several times in the last few years, this Swiss brand founded in 1911 is emerging from an extended bad patch by turning back to the secrets of its winning streak of the 1970s and 1980s: ergonomic sport watches and a few well-conceived mechanical pieces.

After a long period of instability, Ebel is finally seeing the light at the end of the tunnel. In the 1970s, when Pierre-Alain Blum took over the family company founded by his forbears in 1911 in La Chaux-de-Fonds, Switzerland, he brought along an innate understanding of watches as desirable products. In 1977, for instance, he released the Sport Classic, the steel monocoque case watch that introduced the famous "wave" bracelet fated to become the foundation stone of Ebel's expansion. Blum's equally sharp technical know-how soon convinced companies such as Cartier to hire Ebel to construct some its watches. Last but not least, Blum had a flair for public relations: in 1986 he purchased Le Corbusier's Villa Turque in La Chaux-de-Fonds to provide the inspiration for his company's new advertising slogan—"The architects of time." Sure enough, sales took off and before long Ebel was an international player. Yet in 1994, following a failed attempt to diversify outside the timepiece industry, Blum had to sell the brand to Investcorp. Five years later the company changed hands again and became part of the LVMH group. By 2004 LVMH tired of covering Ebel's debts and threw in the towel. The American Movado Group acquired an anemic Ebel, with a muddled image and watches that no longer met the market's expectations. Movado tackled Ebel's problems with a clear strategy: to reestablish the company in the luxury timepiece market by exploiting the models and values integral to its past successes.

Though Ebel has acknowledged that it will take some years for it to return to its peak production of a hundred thousand models a year, or simply break even, there can be no doubt that its collections have already regained their allure. Ebel's catalog has been restructured to center on the brand's emblematic pieces (the Sport Classic, the 1911, and the Beluga), all of which were intelligently reworked but have retained their signature touches (including hexagonal cases, the five-screw bezel, and the wave-shaped bracelet links of the all-steel models). The Classic Wave line has been updated with a thoroughly successful streamlined spin on its iconic design. Now slimmer and more fluid, these ergonomic and elegant quartz watches are a pleasure to wear (starting at $2,000).

In the same family the brand launched the Classic Hexagon line in 2007, consisting of rather sober-looking automatic watches, with a power reserve and retrograde date display (around $5,000).

1911 Tekton.
Automatic chronograph with aperture time display.

1911 BTR.
Automatic chronograph.

1911 BTR Skeleton Chronograph.
Perpetual calendar, moon phases, and automatic movement.

Classic Hexagon.
Automatic watch with power reserve indicator.

Classic Mini.
Ladies' quartz watch.

In addition to this line equipped with subcontracted movements (by ETA and Valjoux), Ebel has developed five calibers unique to its name. Besides an automatic GMT, they are essentially chronographs, and one is combined with a moon-phase perpetual calendar. These highly regarded movements are handsomely crafted and all are certified by the COSC. They outfit the models of the 1911 BTR and 1911 Tekton collections. In addition to a classic automatic chronograph (caliber 137, developed in 1995) offered at an attractive price ($6,950), the brand released a more original and distinguished model in 2008, the 1911 Tekton (caliber 139), where the times measured are no longer displayed by counters, but by an aperture (about $10,000). Finally, soccer fans will be lured by the 1911 Tekton 245, an automatic chronograph designed to measure half-times of matches.

GÉRALD GENTA

COMPLEX AND FANCIFUL

Acquired by the Bulgari Group in 2000, the brand was originally founded in 1969 by designer Gérald Genta, a well-known maverick in the Swiss timepiece business. Famous for its outrageous dials, complicated calibers, jump-hour watches, and retrograde hands (a hand "retrogrades" by jumping back before it displays the following hour, minute, or second), Gérald Genta continues to appeal to timepiece connoisseurs who want to stand out from the crowd.

Though Gérald Genta has long since left the company he founded in 1969, current owner Bulgari has wisely remained faithful to his unconventional spirit. Indeed, Gérald Genta is famous in the world of watches not only for having designed one of the most famous Swiss sport watches of the 1970s—Audemars Piguet's Royal Oak—but also for having graced the same period with an *haute horlogerie* watch featuring Mickey Mouse on its dial. Genta's other mechanical investigations have ranged from the elaboration of a minute repeater caliber barely 1/10th of an inch thick to the conception of highly complicated mechanisms. In 1994, for instance, the company made a stir by introducing its Grande Sonnerie, a wristwatch then considered the most complex in the world. Composed of a thousand parts—and featuring a tourbillon, minute repeater, perpetual calendar, and unique Westminster carillon striking work—the Grande Sonnerie took five years to develop. Two years later, Gérald Genta introduced the Rétro and Bi-Rétro movements. The Rétro combines a jump hour with retrograde minutes, while the Bi-Rétro combines the above functions with a retrograde date display. One of the brand's major specialties is finding ways to tell time in a playful manner, an approach found in various forms throughout its collections (Octo, Arena, and Fantasy), and occasionally coupled with more weighty complications (tourbillon and minute repeater).

Today Gérald Genta produces some 2,500 watches a year and shares manufacturing facilities with the Daniel Roth watch company, which was also acquired by Bulgari in 2000. Ranging in price from $17,400 to more than $910,000, Genta watches continue to demonstrate unfettered creativity in both their design and their mechanisms.

Though most Genta movements are developed from Girard-Perregaux bases, they are fitted with additional high-end modules made in-house, and Genta makes its own movements for all striking work complications. For instance, the wealthy enthusiast is sure to covet the jewel in the Genta crown, an extraordinary Grande Sonnerie with retrograde hours and an updated caliber improved for sturdiness. Aside from its minute repeater function and retrograde hours, the Grande Sonnerie remains the only watch on the market to offer Westminster carillon striking work on four hammers. Plan on spending $910,000 to enjoy its dulcet tones.

Gefica.
Jump-hour watch with retrograde minutes and date.

Octo Minute Repeater.
Minute repeater watch with jump hour and retrograde minutes.

Arena Spice.
Jump-hour watch with retrograde minutes.

Grande Sonnerie.
Watch with carillon striking work, tourbillon, and minute repeater. White gold case.

Octo Ultimate Fantasy.
Automatic tourbillon with retrograde hours.

In 2005 Genta launched a wide range of interesting complications. In the Octo collection, known for garish dials that look carved out of roulette wheels, a new automatic-wound minute repeater with a jump hour and a retrograde minute hand was issued in a limited edition. Even more outlandish, the Octo Ultimate Fantasy, in a limited edition of twenty-five pieces, is an automatic watch with tourbillon and retrograde hours, accompanied by Mickey Mouse on the dial ($179,500).

Equally complex models have recently been issued in the Arena collection, which is also known for its spectacular dials. A prime example is the Arena Chrono Quattro Retro launched in 2005. Its skeleton dial has no less than four retrograde functions, including retrograde chronograph minutes and hours ($56,500). The Arena Spice, a jump-hour watch with retrograde minutes, has a dial that looks like a Vasarely painting ($17,500). Another curiosity, the Gefica, with a bronze case, was created in 1988 to enable hunters to wear a watch off which no light would inadvertently reflect. Its model including jump hour, retrograde minutes and retrograde date is a fine timepiece ($17,400).

Finally, those nostalgic for Mickey Mouse will find their favorite cartoon character on a Gérald Genta dial for a relatively affordable price (just over $10,000). Keep in mind that these hilarious jump-hour models are really only suited for "children" aged thirty and older.

Ellipsocurvex Minute Repeater.
White gold case. Limited edition of 15.

Papillon Chronographe.
With jump hours.

Daniel Roth: Form and Function

Savvy collectors have been aware of Daniel Roth watches since 1989. Roth watches are characterized by masterfully executed, complicated movements and an immediately recognizable shape (truncated oval case and guilloché dial). Daniel Roth, which has been part of the Bulgari Group since 2000, produces 1,500 watches a year, with prices ranging from $14,300 to more than $503,000. The company is perhaps best known for its beautiful tourbillons, which are now entirely produced in-house (Roth previously used Lemania as a supplier). In 2000 Daniel Roth became one of the first companies to issue a tourbillon with an eight-day power reserve. One may prefer the sumptuous Tourbillon Lumière, a skeleton model with manual windup, decorated entirely by hand (limited series of five pieces, $236,000 apiece in pink gold). Another Roth mainstay is the minute repeater. The 2005 Ellipsocurvex contains a hand-wound Daniel Roth caliber (DR750) with a double-gong striking mechanism that provides remarkable sound (issued in a limited edition of fifteen, $256,500 apiece). And don't miss out on the brand's best seller: the Papillon watch with jump hours and retrograde minutes, initially released in 1998. A modernized version of the Papillon appears today in a chronograph model; when the hour jumps, two minute hands briefly appear on a 180-degree dial (about $49,300).

Tourbillon Lumière.
Mechanical skeleton chronograph with manual winding.

GIRARD-PERREGAUX

A PERFECT TRACK RECORD

This Swiss timepiece manufacturer produces sixteen thousand watches per year. The Tourbillon with Three Gold Bridges in the Vintage 1945 line is Girard-Perregaux's trademark product, but the company has not neglected its top-notch sport watches.

Most recently acquired by retired race car driver Luigi Macaluso in 1992, Girard-Perregaux was initially founded in Geneva in 1791. In the mid-nineteenth century the company settled in La Chaux-de-Fonds, Switzerland, and began to establish its reputation as a maker of ultrathin calibers. Toward 1860 the workshop was bought by Constant Girard and his wife, Marie Perregaux. Seven years later Girard invented the Tourbillon with Three Gold Bridges, which uses gold as a functional metal within the movement. Awarded prizes at both the 1867 and 1889 World Fairs in Paris, this technical and aesthetic masterpiece was so strong that by the 1901 fair it was deemed unbeatable, and was classified out of competition.

But it doesn't stop there. Though it is less well known, another of the company's achievements is tremendously important. In 1969 Girard-Perregaux established quartz's oscillation frequency at 33,768 hertz, the frequency that has since served as a standard for every quartz watch in the world. Though the company has now rededicated itself to developing mechanical timepieces, it continues to produce excellent calibers used both in everyday casual models and in timepieces by other luxury watch brands.

Girard-Perregaux wisely invests 10 percent of its annual sales figure in research and development, and has reaped the benefits with a reputation for high-quality, ultrathin (less than 1/10th of an inch thick) automatic movements (GP 3200 and GP 3300); automatic chronograph calibers with column wheels (GP 3080), which are among the most reliable on the market; and, of course, its crown jewel, the highly complicated Tourbillon with Three Gold Bridges. As a highly adaptable manufacturer, Girard-Perregaux produces a wide variety of timepieces, ranging in price from $5,000 to $650,000.

Production of the celebrated Tourbillon with Three Gold Bridges, whose perfectly balanced design clearly distinguishes it as one of the most beautiful tourbillons in the world, is limited to about a hundred pieces per year. In 1981 a replica of the original Tourbillon with Three Gold Bridges was released in a limited edition of twenty pocket watches. The tourbillon is also used in a variety of other Girard-Perregaux models, including a lovely miniature version for women set in a 1.2-inch case in the Cat's Eye line, which starts at $16,990. For men the company released a Tourbillon with Three Gold Bridges with automatic winding (caliber GP 9600) in 1999. It is found notably in the Vintage 1945 line, in a limited edition of fifty launched in 2009—a stunningly beautiful timepiece available for $195,000.

Vintage 1945 XXL.
Tourbillon with Three Gold Bridges.

Vintage Tourbillon Jackpot.
Mechanical tourbillon with slot-machine function and striking mechanism.

1966.
Automatic watch with annual calendar and equation of time.

Vintage 1945.
Automatic watch with small
seconds and date indicator.

ww.TC 24-Hour Shopping.
Universal hour watch with
automatic movement.

Single push-button split-second
chronograph with flying
seconds and tourbillon.

And once this complication is matched with other functions, the pieces in question enter the realm of the truly exceptional watches reserved for extremely wealthy collectors. This is certainly the case with the incredible Vintage 1945 Jackpot Tourbillon, introduced in 2007. Not content with simply providing the time and displaying a tourbillon at six o'clock, this extravagant piece also serves as a slot machine. After five years of development, the watchmaker succeeded in miniaturizing the mechanism of a one-armed bandit. By pulling the lever placed on the side of the case, one can marvel at the three spinning rollers. The jackpot price? $625,000.

On a more classic front, one should mention the Opera Two, with manual winding, Westminster chime minute repeater, and perpetual calendar ($600,000). Or the limited-edition Tourbillon Chronograph introduced in 2008, which combines a tourbillon with a mono push-button chronograph and split-time counter plus a *seconde foudroyante*, or split second—a must-have for those who appreciate measuring time down to 1/6th of a second—available for $530,000.

Aside from these highly complicated watches, of which only a few hundred are issued per year, Girard-Perregaux makes excellent shaped watches such as the Richeville, with a tonneau case (starting at $6,000), and the geometric Vintage 1945 line, which today brings in 30 percent of the brand's annual sales. Its rectangular, arched case, inspired by a 1945 model and redesigned in 2009, incorporates various GP calibers. Aside from the chronograph, worthy of mention is the Vintage 1945 Automatique with small seconds and date display ($7,000). Also well regarded is the very chic Girard-Perregaux 1966 annual calendar with time equation; the round dial provides perfect readability of its functions ($31,000).

In another vein, the house is known for its world time watches (the ww.TC line) that display the time, via a turning bezel, in twenty-four cities of the world. The ww.TC Financial even gives the opening times of the major stock markets ($14,650 in steel), while the ww.TC Lady 24-Hour Shopping gives the main streets of fashion. The price for doing one's shopping with no time lag: $22,750.

DE GRISOGONO

OFFBEAT LUXURY

Occhio Ripetizione Minuti.
Minute repeater with
diaphragm mechanism that
opens the dial when the
minute repeater strikes. Limited
edition of 50.

Meccanico dG.
Dual analog and digital display.

Instrumento N⁰Uno.
Dual time zone watch with
automatic movement and large
date display at 7 o'clock. Rose
gold case.

Initially known for its black-diamond jewelry lines, de Grisogono launched its first watches in 2000. Boasting classy designs, novel materials, and some surprising innovations, the company's watches are indisputably original.

In 2004 Fawaz Gruosi, the CEO and founder of de Grisogono, decided it was time for his company to issue a minute repeater. Gruosi's decision to take on the most prestigious of timepiece complications was not spurred not by a love of the craft but by a taste for challenges. Gruosi wanted to bring a new interpretation to a complication traditionally handled in a very classic manner. A year later the introduction of his Occhio Ripetizione Minuti at the 2005 Basel Watch Fair left timepiece professionals speechless, staring in awe at a watch that looked more like a camera than a timepiece. The Occhio's dial is a diaphragm divided into twelve ceramic shutters that open and close with each strike of the minute repeater, allowing the wearer a glimpse into the mechanical movement designed by the brilliant watchmaker Christophe Claret. This incredible piece single-handedly proved de Grisogono's point that it is possible to radically update Swiss watchmaking, both its design and the actual composition of its movements. Of course the most eloquent argument in de Grisogono's favor is that every one of the fifty limited-edition watches seems to have found a buyer, despite a hefty price tag of $296,800 apiece.

Having made a name for himself in jewelry starting in 1993, the extravagant Fawaz Gruosi took only a few years to impose his style of watchmaking on the world. With a production of a few thousand timepieces a year, de Grisogono now offers about ten lines of watches. Its models are easily recognized by their pronounced style. De Grisogono cases are round, square, or curved, and always voluminous. Dials are finely worked and every detail is meticulously honed. De Grisogono is also notable for issuing several versions of its watches in finishes and materials used in jewelry but rarely found on timepieces (blackened gold, chocolate-colored gold, studding with black diamonds, etc.). In other words, Grisogono has set new standards for luxury watches by giving men the opportunity to express their every whim through a wide range of ultrasophisticated finishes.

Although most de Grisogono movements are subcontracted (ETA, etc.), the brand is known for developing innovative calibers with new functions. Thus, taking up the diaphragm principle of the Occhio, the brand introduced the Fuso Quadrato No1 in 2009: an automatic watch with a dial that opens at leisure onto a second time zone display—a fanciful piece for wealthy travelers at $31,400. Even more spectacular is Meccanico dG No2: an all-mechanical watch with a dual (analog and digital) display. In addition, this

Fuso Quadrato No1.
Automatic watch with diaphragm
mechanism that opens to reveal
a second time zone, shown here
in closed and open positions.

patented caliber contains 651 components and displays two time zones. Count on spending upward of $360,000 to be able to fasten this futuristic watch to your wrist.

As for the more classic pieces, de Grisogono is known for the Instrumento NºUno, the first opus of the brand, launched in 2000. It offers two special features: a dual time zone and an oversize date display at half past seven o'clock. The price for this automatic piece starts in the neighborhood of $23,100. Or there is the Instrumento Novantatre, an automatic annual calendar (starting around $13,000) released in 2007. Finally, in 2006 the brand introduced a playful large-date display, the Grand Open Date No7, with an original design that shows the integration of both plates of the perpetual calendar on the dial ($28,600).

GUCCI

A STYLISH BRAND

Twirl.
Quartz watch with moving dial.

Marina Chain.
Quartz watch with brilliant-cut diamond markers.

Signoria.
Quartz watch with malachite dial, diamond-set case.

Some consider that Gucci invented the fashion watch—or, rather, that its talented licensee, Severin Wunderman, invented it. Wunderman (who died in 2008) obtained the license to manufacture timepieces for the famous Florentine luggage maker in the early 1970s. By carrying the emblematic Gucci designs and colors over to watches, he succeeded not only in creating a new concept—watches became fashion accessories just like scarves and bags—but in pulling off one of the tidiest financial operations of the era. By the 1980s Gucci was selling up to a million watches a year. Despite being copied in record numbers, these watches were the motor for one of the most profitable timepiece production and distribution enterprises in the world.

Finally, in the early twenty-first century, Gucci Group (which now belongs to PPR) paid an arm and a leg to acquire Severin Wunderman's company. End of act one. With production increasing to several hundred thousand pieces per year, Gucci today faces steep competition from other fashion houses now established in the timepiece business. Nevertheless, the Italian company remains a standard for anyone in search of a relatively affordable high-quality designer watch. Gucci's timepiece collection consists of numerous models, virtually always quartz, all Swiss made. The watches elegantly reproduce the signature touches that made the Florentine saddler famous (red and green, the horse bit, the Flora print, the double G, the anchor chain, etc.). Witness the Twirl cuff watch, with a movable case and a steel bracelet that effectively showcases the Florentine colors ($650). Also of note is the Marina Chain, with anchor chain links that are timeless ($935 in stainless steel with diamonds). Other perennially Italian watches include the G Chrono, released in 2005 ($1,795), and the I-Gucci, a rather well-designed watch with a digital display ($1,295).

HAMILTON

THE SPIRIT OF AMERICA

Slim.
Automatic watch with
date display.

Khaki Base Jump.
Automatic chronograph with
push buttons incorporated into
the bezel.

Elvis Presley wore one on-screen in *Blue Hawaii*. Thousands of GIs, including John F. Kennedy, wore them on the battlefield. Today Hamilton is probably the only American brand in the Swatch Group to capitalize on its history. Founded in Lancaster, Pennsylvania, in 1892, the company has long been on the frontlines of American history: it constructed pocket watches for the railroads, was the official watchmaker for GIs during World War II (the famous Khaki watches), launched the first electric watch in 1957 (the Ventura), and is now the brand most frequently spotted in Hollywood blockbusters.

Though famous in the United States—where its models were made until production was moved to Switzerland in 2002—Hamilton has had a hard time finding a niche for its hundreds of thousands of watches on the French market. Some blame the company for trying to pattern its offerings too much after those of other companies. Yet the fact remains that with more than half a dozen different lines, Hamilton has a lot going for it. Their vintage designs, the Classic line, are without contest the most well made, and their general price range (between $600 and $1,800) is affordable. On top of that, the majority of Hamilton's timepieces are equipped with solid ETA automatic movements. Among the most interesting models, the Khaki Base Jump, unveiled at the 2009 Basel Watch Fair, is distinctive for its integration of the chronograph push-button functions into the bezel of the watch. This is patented by Hamilton, developed with an automatic movement based on the Valjoux 7750 ($1,245). Another Hamilton classic, the Ventura, with a snazzy "electrified" case worn by Elvis Presley, has given rise to a variety of men's and ladies' models. To celebrate the seventy-fifth birthday of the King, Hamilton is releasing a redesigned model that will only be sold from September 2009 to December 2010. The result is the automatic Ventura XXL, black and distinctly more contemporary ($1,195). In 2005 Hamilton introduced the Jazzmaster line of elegant round watches with a striking 1950s feel. The best models are the Jazzmaster chronograph and the Jazzmaster with power reserve indication. Both are automatic pieces available for about $950. The Slim, a classic watch released in 2009, is not bad either; with a simple automatic movement, three hands and date, it retails in the neighborhood of $800.

Ventura XXL Elvis.
Automatic watch.

HERMÈS

CHIC TIME

With some hundred thousand models sold a year, the Parisian saddler has carved itself a choice position in the world of ladies' watches. Though the majority of its collections consist of quartz watches, in 2003 Hermès ventured into the world of mechanical timepieces by inaugurating the Dressage line equipped with Vaucher movements. Definitely worth keeping an eye on.

At first glance Hermès watches convey an impression of serenity. Their cases are harmonious, their bracelets unostentatious, and their movements accurate. The brand's sixteen timepiece collections flout the latest fashions in favor of the company's illustrious heritage, with consistent references to leather and the world of horseback riding.

Hermès embarked on the watch business in 1928 with the release of the Ermeto, the first watch bearing the Hermès name. This pocket watch equipped with a Movado movement was wound by opening and closing leather-covered sliding shells. Until the late 1970s Hermès hired great Swiss manufacturers such as Universal or Jaeger-LeCoultre to produce its timepiece collections, but in 1978 the company finally created its own timepiece division in Bienne, Switzerland. Today Hermès's timepiece division produces a hundred thousand watches a year, and accounts for between 6 percent and 8 percent of the company's sales figure.

Hermès models are generally made for women and predominantly equipped with quartz movements. Among the more interesting pieces in this range, one should mention the Kelly, created in 1975. The Kelly case was initially inspired by the lock on the celebrated Hermès bag of the same name and has since been produced in several different versions (starting at $1,625). The Médor, whose dog-collar bracelet conceals a silver dial, is equally characteristic of the Hermès flair ($2,750 for stainless steel).

Hermès's unisex collections include the brand's best seller, the relatively sporty Clipper, but most notable is the Heure H, featuring a case in the shape of an H (from $1,475). The Cape Cod is another fine representative of the Hermès style. Though it was launched in 1991, the Cape Cod didn't really take off until 1998, when Martin Margiela, the brand's head designer at the time, came up with the idea of equipping it with a double-wrap strap. Note that Hermès is one of the only brands in the world to manufacture its own watchstraps. In any case, the double-wrap strap was such a success that it set off a veritable chain reaction of imitations, none of which equaled the original. In short, the Cape Cod is a naturally elegant watch also offered, since 2009, in a extremely well-crafted tonneau model—true Parisian chic, available for $2,250.

So much for style. Turning to content, it should be mentioned that over the years the brand has expanded its range of mechanical timepieces. Having already added auto-

Cape Cod Grandes Heures.
Automatic watch with variable-speed hour hands.

Dressage.
Automatic watch with petpetual calendar and moon phase.

Cape Cod Tonneau.
Quartz watch.

Arceau.
Automatic watch with date display.

Kelly Clochette.
Quartz watch. Yellow-gold case housed in a pendant.

Clipper H1 Grande Date.
Automatic watch with date display.

matic models to preexisting collections (Arceau, Cape Cod, Clipper, etc.), in 2006 Hermès acquired a 25 percent share of the capital of Vaucher Manufacture Fleurier, a Swiss company specializing in high-performance calibers. Moreover, it was Vaucher that in 2003 introduced the first Hermès watch to specifically target horology connoisseurs. Named Dressage, this automatic in-house caliber simply displays the date and is characterized by a cushion case and circled markers. In 2004 this line grew to include a moon phase model, once again developed with the Vaucher workshop ($34,475). An annual calendar was added in 2008 ($39,590 in rose gold) and a perpetual calendar in 2009 ($57,000). They are pieces that, by the level of their finishing quality, may rival certain mechanical Swiss watches.

In the same horological spirit, Hermès has for some years been working with Vaucher to develop its first automatic movement, the H1: a double barrel caliber with engraved large date display to durably outfit its best sellers (Cape Cod, Clipper, etc.). This Grandes Heures module, which any watchmaker had only dreamed of until its arrival, operates by virtue of a sophisticated system of oval cogwheels that enable the acceleration or deceleration of the hour hands without affecting the rhythm of the minutes or the seconds. The effect is visually stunning: between certain hours the hour hands no longer circle the dial in their usual, sensible pattern, but instead compose their own new choreography inspired by poetry and fancy.

HUBLOT

RUBBER AND GOLD

Big Bang.
Automatic chronograph with red gold and tantalum case. Limited edition of 250.

Big Bang King.
Diving watch water resistant to 984 feet, automatic movement.

Bigger Bang All Black.
Mechanical chronograph with tourbillon and manual winding. Limited edition of 50.

Launched in 1980 by a Milan watchmaker eager to create a watch that could be worn for every occasion, Hublot was the first watch in the history of watchmaking to be equipped with a natural rubber strap. Nearly thirty years later the brand revitalized its concept by fusing new materials in a series of interesting chronographs.

The first Hublot watch was introduced at the Basel Watch Fair in 1980. Featuring a yellow-gold case inspired by a ship's porthole, with twelve titanium screws for markers, a black natural rubber strap, a quartz movement and, in a total break with the codes of classic watchmaking, a design stripped of any embellishments, the Hublot immediately set off a scandal. To make matters worse, this Carlo Crocco creation drew the ire of the Swiss brands by positioning itself as a luxury watch. In the first year of distribution, Crocco sold only five thousand Hublot watches. Five years later, he sold fifty thousand. The Hublot became the watch of choice for European royalty. From Constantine of Greece to Juan Carlos of Spain, no monarch could resist the extravagant combination of gold and rubber, the encounter between a noble metal and a material so unlikely it seemed cutting-edge. In 1987–88 the Milanese brand expanded on the single product concept by introducing its first self-wound models followed by a series of chronographs. Throughout the 1990s the Hublot case and its famous strap were matched with dual time zone, date display, power reserve, and diving functions, and released in limited editions featuring enamel dials and engraved lids decorated with precious stones. But in the meantime, Hublot was facing competition from other companies that had started to invest in rubber. In the early twenty-first century, Hublot's grip on the European markets slackened, except in Spain, where it remained the second most popular watch brand.

Jean-Claude Biver's 2004 appointment as CEO reinvigorated the company. Renowned for having jump-started Blancpain in the 1980s, Biver set to work brushing away the cobwebs by revamping Hublot's fundamental principles. Biver launched the "fusion" concept by combining traditional timepiece elements with innovative materials (gold with Kevlar, ceramic with rubber, etc.). Named the Hublot Big Bang, this new opus got off to a great start at the 2005 Basel Watch Fair, attracting a younger clientele. This best seller put Hublot back on track for economic growth and, especially, pushed up prices, from $6,500 (for the classic Hublot in zirconium) to $11,900 (for a Big Bang chronograph in steel and ceramic). With current production at about twenty-six thousand watches a year, Hublot was bought in 2008 by LVMH.

Betting on a monoproduct strategy, Hublot now bases virtually all its offerings on the Big Bang. Highly recommended, this chronograph is available starting at $11,900 in

King Power.
Automatic chronograph with flying seconds. Limited edition of 500.

Big Bang Aero Bang.
Automatic chronograph. Limited edition of 500.

steel. Its greatest appeal lies in its case, which is composed of fourteen parts (as opposed to the three on a standard case) arranged in a sandwich structure. Viewing the Big Bang from the side reinforces the multilayered feel created by a Kevlar insert that also makes it the first watch featuring lateral recognition. This "fusion" of materials is available in an impressive number of options cut from classic and/or unconventional materials: rose gold, steel, titanium, magnesium, and zirconium cases; carbon fiber dials; ceramic bezels; bracelets in plain rubber or mixed with ceramic links. This sleek chronograph is equipped with a La Joux-Perret automatic movement and offers models in a variety of colors and stones for women, and is enriched each year with limited series. Take, for example, the Big Bang All Black II in ceramic black, the first watch in history designed like a monochromatic Soulages painting, where the time (quasi-invisible) becomes secondary ($8,900, limited series of 250 pieces). Another curiosity is the One Million Dollar Big Bang, with a white-gold case that completely disappears underneath an avalanche of baguette diamonds. Unveiled in 2007, this unique piece was sold for $1 million. Within the same family, in addition to the diving models housed in extralarge 1.88-inch cases and waterproof to 984 feet (the Big Bang King, which sells for $26,900 in palladium), the brand began developing truly contemporary pieces with tourbillons in 2006. They are coupled with a chronograph (the Bigger Bang All Black for $220,000) or a large date display (the Big Date Black ceramic for $125,000). More recently, Hublot unveiled timepieces with skeleton-like cutout dials, such as the Aéro Bang chronograph in tungsten, which leaves the black inner workings exposed and sells for $19,900.

Finally, the company launched its latest opus at the 2009 Basel Watch Fair: the King Power, presented as the crowning achievement of the Big Bang. Larger, more powerful, more rugged than its predecessor, this watch seems steeped in testosterone and is available in rose gold, zirconium, or ceramic. Equipped with a chronograph with a split-time counter and a split-second movement from La Joux-Perret, it can be had for $33,500 in gold. In conclusion, 2010 should see the birth of the first caliber manufactured by Hublot: an automatic chronograph with visible column wheels on the dial, a split-time counter, a fly-back and dual gears—one for the hours, the other for the minutes. It should be good.

IWC

AESTHETICS AND TECHNIQUE

This manufacturer, founded in 1868 by an American in German-speaking Switzerland, is famous for complicated pieces such as perpetual calendars. It is also admired for the technical proficiency evident in watches such as the Portuguese, which can be as beautiful to look at as they are technically dazzling.

IWC has been on a roll for the past several years. According to the CEO, the company produces between sixty and eighty thousand watches annually. The brand's models draw enthusiasts thanks to their sober design; straightforward, easy-to-use functions; high-quality movements; and still-tolerable prices (the average price for an IWC is between $10,000 and $20,000).

Owned by the Richemont luxury group since 2000, the International Watch Company was originally founded in Schaffhausen by American businessman Florentine Ariosto Jones. Despite Jones's savvy objective to make quality Swiss watches for the American market, the company filed for bankruptcy twice and was eventually taken over by a local industrialist. Following the takeover, IWC began making pocket watches with digital displays based on the Pallweber system, then turned its attention to making pilot watches in the 1930s. Now highly sought-after by collectors, these pilot wristwatches (the Mark IX, X, and XI) are characterized by a large dial and robust movements, some of which are equipped with an antimagnetic system. In 1938 IWC developed what would become its best seller: the Portuguese, a watch conceived to satisfy two Portuguese tradesmen's request for a wristwatch with a highly accurate pocket-watch caliber. In the 1950s IWC's automatic movements were improved with the Pellaton winding mechanism, a patented automatic winding system that limited energy loss by replacing traditional gears.

After releasing several innovative pieces on the sport watch market (the Aquatimer, water-resistant to 650 feet, in 1967; the first titanium watches, for A. F. Porsche, in 1980), IWC embarked on producing complicated timepieces with the 1985 launch of the Da Vinci. The Da Vinci was the first self-wound chronograph wristwatch to have a perpetual calendar mechanically programmed for the next five hundred years and to indicate the current year in four digits. It also featured an accurate moon phase display that only varies every 120 years and, to top it all off, was available in a ceramic case.

The no-hassle, user-friendly perpetual calendar has since become one of IWC's specialties. It can be found on the Grande Complication, a self-wound automatic chronograph that doubles as a minute repeater and is produced in a limited run of fifty pieces a year ($240,000 in rose gold). The perpetual calendar is also available in the Da Vinci line, which underwent a complete makeover in 2007. Its new barrel-shaped case now incorporates a perpetual calendar in the Kurt Klaus limited edition and in the especially interesting Da Vinci Digital.

Da Vinci.
Automatic chronograph with perpetual calendar, and month-date display.

Aquatimer Deep Two.
Automatic diving watch with mechanical depth gauge.

Big Pilot's Watch.
Automatic watch with 7-day power reserve. Steel case.

Portuguese Perpetual Calendar.
Mechanical watch with
perpetual calendar and
moon phase.

Big Ingénieur.
Automatic chronograph with
fly-back function.

Released in 2009, this automatic perpetual calendar chronograph digitally displays on its dial the date, the month and the leap years in separate apertures and goes for $44,300 in rose gold. Also of note is the Da Vinci, with an automatic caliber manufactured by IWC with a price of $5,800 in steel.

Emblematic of the IWC style, the Portuguese is highly recommendable. This flagship line keeps on growing, and the workshop has developed a large new automatic caliber, the IWC C.5000, with a seven-day power reserve and a Pellaton winding mechanism, in order to have a reliable base to conceive new complication modules. The Portuguese Perpetual Calendar clearly exhibits this commitment to breathtaking complications. Aside from the calendar and a seven-day power reserve, the watch provides a new, patented moon phase indication for both hemispheres that varies by just 1 day every 577 years, making it even more accurate than the Da Vinci. This magnificent specimen is available in rose gold with a black dial for $31,500. The Portuguese line's other complications include, notably, a Tourbillon Mystère ($94,000 in rose gold), a Minute Repeater ($77,000 in rose gold), and a Regulateur ($11,000 in stainless steel). Less extravagant but just as pretty, the classic Portuguese can be had in an automatic chronograph model for $6,800 in stainless steel. A little more expensive, the basic automatic model, with a small second hand, date display, and seven-day power reserve, is available for $18,600 in rose gold.

IWC also produces a collection of pilot watches such as the Spitfire chronographs. The most famous is the Big Pilot's Watch, a replica of a 1930s model featuring an oversize case (1.82 inches in diameter) fitted with the workshop's seven-day power reserve automatic caliber. In a spirit that is just as retro, the watchmaker came out with the Vintage Collection to celebrate its fortieth anniversary in 2008: it includes the rerelease of six IWC icons (the Portuguese, Aviator, Da Vinci, Ingénieur, Portofino, and Aquatimer) at prices ranging from $7,300 to $10,900 for the models in steel. On a more athletic front, in 2009 IWC revamped its line of diving watches. The result is five new pieces with a peppier design. The Aquatimer Deep Two is equipped with a mechanical depth gauge that measures up to 164 feet and is priced at $15,600 for stainless steel. The Aquatimer Chronograph model in rose gold is equipped with the in-house movement and is available for $19,900. At $4,400, the Aquatimer Automatic 2000, with 3 hands and water-resistance to 656 feet, offers a good quality-to-price ratio.

Finally, in the Ingénieur family, released in 2005 on the occasion of IWC's partnership with the German builder Mercedes-AMG, we note the arrival of a model boasting a more ample case (1.79 inches), which sells for $25,700 in rose gold. These sport watches are equipped with IWC's nonmagnetic automatic caliber 80110 and a shock-absorption system. The Ingénieur is one of the most muscular automatic watches on the market. Unfortunately its design is not as innovative as its movement.

JAEGER-LECOULTRE

MANUFACTURING TIME

Master Control.
Automatic movement.

Master Minute Repeater.
Mechanical watch with manual
winding.

Calibers produced in-house from the first step to the last, timeless collections, consistent quality from basic movements to the most complicated models, and more than 170 years of experience: can one really blame the French for worshipping Jaeger-LeCoultre watches?

Antoine LeCoultre founded his "farm-workshop" in the Joux Valley of the Swiss Jura, in 1833. The man who would eventually be considered the "grandfather of horology" specialized in high-end calibers, which he sold both under his own name and to other brands. In 1890 the company made a modest 125 movements. Yet in the years since, all the great names in watchmaking, from Audemars Piguet to Patek Philippe, from Cartier to Vacheron Constantin, have lined up to buy movements from LeCoultre at one time or another.

This is hardly surprising, given the company's track record: 1,247 calibers developed over the course of its history, more than 300 patents filed since 1888, and numerous unbeatable records—including, in 1903, the thinnest watch movement in the world (0.072 inches); in 1929, the 101 caliber, the smallest mechanical movement in the world; and, in 1982, the 601 caliber, the smallest quartz movement (0.07 inches). Jaeger-LeCoultre also boasts legendary pieces such as the Atmos clock, which draws power from temperature variations and has not required winding since it was manufactured in 1928, or the Reverso, created in 1931 by Edmond Jaeger, with a case that could be rotated inward to allow British army officers in India to play polo without damaging their precious timepieces. Aside from the classic model with automatic winding (about $5,000), the large dual-time Reverso with an eight-day power reserve is remarkable for its combination of a balanced aesthetic, excellent caliber, and fair price ($13,000). In 2006 this family grew larger with the Reverso Squadra, a sportier line of three automatic models equipped with GMT functions.

Today the vast Jaeger-LeCoultre factory in Le Sentier employs a thousand people and produces fifty thousand pieces per year. From the case to the wristband, everything is conceived, cut, assembled, and tested in-house. Jaeger-LeCoultre has belonged to the Richemont group since 2001 and therefore enjoys the luxury of being one of the last Swiss watch manufacturers to preserve the coherence of collections while growing them intelligently. For instance, the Master Control line's round watches, which are tested for a thousand hours, are a judicious counterpoint to the Reverso line. In fact, the many Master Control timepieces (which include automatics, ultrathins, chronographs, alarms, perpetual calendars, dual time zone, etc.) now account for more than half of the company's revenue. Of note is the basic automatic model with date (caliber JL 899), which has an excellent price-quality ratio at $7,100 for the steel version. On a sportier front, in 2007 the company launched the Master Compressor Diving line: diving watches water resistant to

Master Compressor Diving
Chronograph GMT Navy SEALs.
Automatic chronograph with
dual time zones, water resistant
to 3,280 feet.

Reverso Tryptique.
Grand complication watch with three dials activated by a single mechanical caliber.

Reverso Grande GMT.
Mechanical dual time zone watch with two back-to-back dials and an 8-day power reserve. Steel case.

Reverso Gyrotourbillon 2.
Mechanical watch with manual winding and spherical tourbillon, shown here front and back.

approximately 3,280 feet, with one model equipped with a manual depth gauge.

Though it is terrifically successful (forty-eight thousand pieces sold in 2005), Jaeger-LeCoultre has not let itself get uppity. (But could one really have blamed Jaeger-LeCoultre's craftsmen for displaying a little pride upon hearing the crystalline sound of the Master Minute Repeater Antoine LeCoultre?) Officially praised by the Basel Watch Fair in 2005, this little treasure's chime was designed in collaboration with orchestra conductor George Prêtre. For the first time in the history of timepieces, there was a minute repeater wristwatch using solid transmission (the sound is carried by a material, rather than through air) to strike at fifty-five decibels across a rich scale of seven partials. Each of the two hundred pieces in this limited edition is being sold for $190,000. Another flagship piece is the Gyrotourbillon I, which required eight years of development. Unveiled in 2004, the Gyrotourbillon is a wristwatch with a tourbillon composed of two frames, each of which turns on its own axis. To make everything a little more complicated, this collector's piece with a five-hundred-part movement is also a perpetual calendar and displays a "running" equation of time. In 2008 the watchmaker launched the Reverso Gyrotourbillon 2, which has been the object of five patents, to obtain an accuracy ten times greater than chronometric standards. This tourbillon has a frame that turns in all directions and is stunningly beautiful (for $370,000)! Even more spectacular is the unequaled Reverso Tryptique: the first watch in the world to have three dials run by a single unique movement. This horological triptych with nineteen complications and eight hundred components was introduced in 2006, in a limited edition of seventy-five pieces, for nearly $500,000.

Another amazing piece introduced in 2007 is the Master Compressor Extreme LAB, not only the first oil-free mechanical watch but one that promises to run forever. This piece, at about $240,000, is horologically ahead of its time, adding to the forty calibers manufactured by this company, which has as one of its mottos: "For Jaeger-LeCoultre, achieving the impossible is the norm."

The Smallest Caliber in the World

The naked eye may be enough to tell you that it's less than half the size of a match, but to really appreciate the finesse of its skeleton, you'll have to use a magnifying glass. Created by Jaeger-LeCoultre in 1929, the 101 Caliber remains the smallest automatic winding mechanical movement in the world. It may be small, but the greats of this world have certainly taken notice of it. Elizabeth II of England, for instance, was wearing the miniature timepiece when she was crowned. In fact, she was wearing her third 101 Caliber, because at that point she had already lost two. In her defense, it should be mentioned that the timepiece in question really is minuscule (0.55 by 0.18 by 0.13 inches), and an authentic featherweight (1 gram). Today only two watchmakers master the art of assembling the eighty-eight pieces that make up the 101 Caliber, a process that generally takes a week. Production of the 101 is in keeping with its caliber. In other words, it is minimal, with only about thirty movements finished per year. The 101's price, however, is inversely proportionate to its size, given that you'll have to shell out at least $29,000 for the chance to wear one.

Jaeger-LeCoultre Joaillerie Rivière 101.

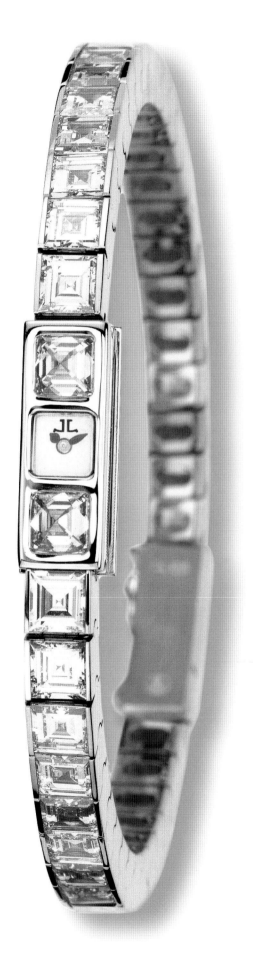

JAQUET DROZ

Date Astrale.
Automatic watch indicating one of the 12 constellations in the zodiac.

Grande Seconde.
Self-winding mechanical movement.

Les 12 Villes.
Automatic jump-hour watch with time indications for 12 cities.

Chrono Monopoussoir.
Mono push-button automatic-chronograph.

MECHANICAL POETRY

There's something undeniably poetic about Jaquet Droz watches. Maybe it's those peaceful slate gray or *grand feu* aventurine enamel dials; or those off-center hour, minute, and second rings that occasionally come together to form a large figure eight. Or maybe it's the finely crafted oscillating weight one discovers upon inspecting the back of a Jaquet Droz case. In any event, Jaquet Droz scales the heights of aesthetic refinement. The brand recently succeeded in imposing its own style, following its takeover by the Swatch Group in 2000.

The company's roots go back to one of the greatest eighteenth-century watch-makers, Pierre Jaquet Droz. Jaquet Droz, who opened his first workshop in La Chaux-de-Fonds in 1738, was celebrated for his richly enameled musical watches and, especially, for the doll-like automata he exhibited throughout the royal courts of Europe. Though the company no longer makes automata, its timepiece collections continue to draw on the heritage of the founding father. With a dozen different models manufactured in small production runs (the company's many limited editions are issued in series of eight pieces or in a run that ends in the number eight—a symbol of good luck in Asia), Jaquet Droz primarily appeals to collectors in search of unusual timepieces. Nearly all of the company's watches feature self-wound, double barrel movements combined with a few complications (perpetual calendar, equation of time, tourbillon, minute repeater, etc.).

The most emblematic Jaquet Droz watch is the Grande Seconde, with a dial inspired by a 1785 pocket watch. This stunningly rarefied timepiece is known for its large, overlapping second and hour rings and retails for $17,900. Among the more complicated models, Jaquet Droz launched an interesting piece in 2008 with astral date and the twelve zodiac signs appearing in a constellation that lights up at night. One should also mention the Chrono Monopoussoir (single push button), which is one of the few timepieces to feature a chronograph hour counter along with an off-center hours/minutes display ($29,000), and the Douze Villes—a jump-hour watch displaying the time in twelve cities around the world ($23,500). A must for the wealthy traveler.

F.-P. JOURNE

EXQUISITE CALIBER

In a span of just a few years, this ex-restorer of antique timepieces from Marseilles has become the prodigy of Swiss *haute horlogerie*. Journe makes only nine hundred watches a year, every one of which is avidly snapped up by collectors.

François-Paul Journe describes himself as a "constructor." He declares that the only thing that interests him is to measure time or, rather, to be able to measure it more accurately. Yet he detests quartz watches and only produces unabashedly unique mechanical calibers whose accuracy and beauty go uncertified by any official body. The COSC and the Poinçon de Genève don't mean a thing to François-Paul Journe: his "chronometers," as he calls them, are enough to make him, and the collectors, happy.

The career of the boy wonder born in Marseilles in 1957 began in Paris in the late 1970s. Following his graduation from the Paris School of Watchmaking, Journe took a job with his uncle, a restorer of antique clocks, and became fixated with the idea of constructing his first watch in the style of the great eighteenth-century watchmakers. In 1982, after five years of hard work, Journe finished the No. 1, a tourbillon pocket watch from another era. The No. 1 was so stunningly made that the International Museum of Horology in La Chaux-de-Fonds put it on display. Three years later Journe set up his own company and got to work conceiving his second opus (the Planetary pocket watch), restoring antique clocks, and building custom pieces. He spent the next ten years devising unique timepieces for individual customers and exclusive calibers for leading Swiss brands. In 1999 he introduced his Invenit et Fecit (Invented and Made) line of wristwatches signed F.-P. Journe with the stated objective of recovering the authenticity of mechanical watch construction while improving it with technical innovations. On both aesthetic and technical levels, Journe's watches are remarkably unique objects that carry the spirits of great watchmakers like Abraham-Louis Breguet or Antide Janvier into the twenty-first century.

Collectors were quick to catch on to Journe's genius. He has become something of a demigod in Japan, the United States, and Switzerland, the countries where he sells most of his annual production at an average price of $46,000 apiece. Journe is also distinct in that he runs one of the few independent brands in the watch industry. In 2003 he inaugurated his Geneva factory, which employs forty-five people, including twenty-three watchmakers. In the workshop, every single component that goes into one of Journe's exquisite calibers is minutely considered to provide optimum running and chronometry. Eighty percent of manufacturing is done in-house in Geneva, including since 2006 the watch's spirals, which are essential to a movement's accuracy. Only cases, hands, rubies, and mainsprings are purchased from other companies. Another

Souverain Chronometer.
Hand-wound mechanical watch. Platinum case.

Resonance Chronometer.
Hand-wound mechanical watch. Platinum case.

Octa Power Reserve.
Automatic watch with power reserve of 120 hours and platinum case.

Sonnerie Souveraine.
Mechanical watch with *grande sonnerie* and minute repeater.

Tourbillon Souverain.
Tourbillon watch with a constant force device.

Centigraphe Souverain.
Manually wound mechanical chronograph that measures 1/100th of a second as 10 minutes.

Journe specialty is that its calibers are no longer made of brass, as is the practice with all other companies, but of red gold in order to improve the operation of certain parts and, especially, to provide more solid components.

Today the Journe collection consists of ten models divided between the hand-wound Souverain line and the self-winding Octa line. The technical prowess on display in all ten of these models has been recognized by numerous watchmaking prizes, including the 2004 Grand Prix d'Horlogerie de Genève, awarded to the Souverain Tourbillon. With this masterpiece, F.-P. Journe met the challenge of fitting a highly complex tourbillon with a *remontoir d'égalité*, or constant-force device, invented in the sixteenth century to ensure constant power to the movement. The Souverain Tourbillon is also the first wristwatch with independent, or deadbeat, seconds, which provide a more accurate reading of the time by remaining motionless ("dead") until the second has actually elapsed. Another emblematic Journe piece, the Chronomètre à Résonance, features a watchmaking specialization forgotten since the eighteenth century and is priced at $82,400. The system improves timekeeping accuracy through two independent balance wheels that vibrate at the same frequency to counteract any exterior disturbance likely to have an impact on the movement. The Octa line features a whole range of complication watches (moon phase, fly-back chronograph, annual calendar, and power reserve) developed on the base of an automatic caliber that can run 120 hours without being worn. The line's best seller is the Octa power reserve.

In addition to the ultrathin Répétition Souveraine with a movement barely 0.157 inches thick, which retails for $165,400, Journe released the sensational Sonnerie Souveraine: a complication distinguished by its ease of use. "I wanted an eight-year-old child to be able to use it without damaging it; that was my challenge," he explained. Mission accomplished with this piece, a *grande sonnerie* with a minute repeater. After six years of development, it has been the object of ten patents. It was crowned with the Aiguille d'Or (the Golden Hand award) at the Grand Prix d'Horlogerie de Genève in 2006. Two years later the watchmaker picked up the Geneva prize once again with the Centigraphe Souverain. This exceptional piece is the first wristwatch in the world equipped with a mechanical movement that allows for measuring 1/100th of a second as 10 minutes (around $61,900). Neophytes will no doubt prefer the Chronomètre Souverain, which, in a marked change for the house of Journe, has only one function, telling time . . . for $34,200.

A. LANGE & SÖHNE

Tourbograph "Pour le Mérite."
Chronograph with split seconds
and a tourbillon.

Lange 31 Jours.
Mechanical watch with a power
reserve of 31 days.

Lange Double Split.
Mechanical chronograph, fly-
back function and double split-
second. Platinum case.

THE REVIVAL OF FINE GERMAN MECHANICS

Among connoisseurs, A. Lange & Söhne is probably one of the most highly regarded watch brands. It is also one of the most elite, for only a trained eye can appreciate the technical superiority of its calibers and the rigorous design of its models. A. Lange & Söhne watches have definitively ushered in the revival of German *haute horlogerie.*

Contrary to popular perception, Switzerland is not the only manufacturer of top-notch timepieces. In the nineteenth century, a high-end German timepiece industry sprang up in the Dresden area thanks to the efforts of a single man, Ferdinand Adolphe Lange, who had been charged in 1845 with transforming the small mining town of Glashütte into the center of the watch business in Saxony. Lange oversaw the opening of many Glashütte workshops before creating his own in 1868. Over the next thirty years, Glashütte became the capital of German precision watchmaking, with A. Lange & Söhne as its finest representative. In 1945 Allied bombing raids destroyed Dresden and Glashütte. In 1951, the area fell under Communist rule and the watch factories were seized and nationalized. After the fall of the Berlin wall, one of Ferdinand Adolphe Lange's descendants, Walter Lange, returned to Glashütte to manufacture high-end movements with all the signature touches of the German craft of watchmaking: three-quarter plates to improve the caliber's stability, gold settings for the movement's rubies, hand-engraved balance components, and precious metal cases and dials.

The first models from the revived A. Lange & Söhne workshop were launched in 1994 with innovations that immediately set the Swiss watch industry abuzz. The mechanism of the Tourbillon "Pour le Mérite," for instance, was conceived to transmit power to the movement more consistently than a traditional tourbillon's. The miniaturizing of this system—known as fusée-chain transmission (chain-driven pulley) and notably employed by Leonardo da Vinci—is testimony to the exceptional craftsmanship of the watchmaker. Collectors raced to get their hands on this limited edition of 150 gold pieces and 50 platinum ones. The equally emblematic Lange 1 introduced an aperture with an oversize date display four times larger than the date on a standard watch. This patented invention was backed by a double barrel mechanism providing the watch with a seventy-two-hour power reserve. In 2005 the line was updated by adding a small complication with the Lange 1 Dual Time Zone, featuring a second time zone and day/night indication with prices ranging from $37,800 to $53,700. It is now the company's best-selling timepiece.

The above models established Lange's brand identity and proved the company could provide aficionados with rigorous designs featuring simple, legible dials and

Lange 1.
Mechanical watch with large
date display in an aperture.
Gold case.

Richard Lange
"Pour Le Mérite."
Mechanical watch with a fusee-
chain transmission.

Lange Zeitwerk.
Mechanical watch with jump
hours and minutes, small
seconds, and power reserve
indicator.

movements built in the tradition of fine German watchmaking. To top it off, Lange watches are innovative, solid, and precisely set.

Having entered the Richemont group in 2000, A. Lange & Söhne now produces roughly five thousand watches a year. Lange's sparing production is based on a selection of twenty-eight calibers, some of which were developed by Renaud & Papi. In keeping with the brand's image, the Lange collection is concise. It includes "simple" watches with time and large date and more complex pieces such as the perpetual calendar, the moon phase, and the tourbillon. Prices start at $15,900 for the hand-wound Saxonia.

Among the more notable Lange pieces, one should mention the Datograph, one of the most legible chronographs in the field, with a variety of price points from $50,900 to $160,400. This hand-wound mechanical piece (caliber L 951.1) has a fly-back function and a precision jumping minute counter. The 2004 hand-wound Double Split boasts yet another Lange novelty: it is the first chronograph equipped with a double rattrapante comprising a seconds counter and a minutes counter, both of which have fly-back functions. When the stopwatch function is in use, the split minute counter can record measurements lasting up to thirty minutes. Last but certainly not least, the Double Split's spiral balance was manufactured by Lange, in Glashütte, a particularly noteworthy achievement given that 99 percent of these essential mechanical watch components are now manufactured by the Swatch Group. Sadly, the Double Split's technical prowess doesn't come cheap. Plan on spending $126,000 for platinum.

Even more complex is the Tourbograph "Pour le Mérite," introduced in 2005: this collector's timepiece is the first tourbillon wristwatch in the world with a fusée-chain transmission that is coupled with a split-time counter chronograph. The brand has produced only forty such pieces, at $460,000 a piece in platinum. In a "simplified" model, A. Lange and Söhne introduced its celebrated fusée-chain transmission system in 2009 in the Richard Lange "Pour le Mérite": a three-hand watch that simply keeps time with remarkable accuracy—with a price tag of $128,600 in platinum.

Finally of note is the Cabaret Tourbillon, which is the only tourbillon in the world to be equipped with a stop-second in order to stop and to restart it at leisure, available for $235,600 in rose gold. Also, the Lange 31, with its spectacular power reserve of thirty-one days, enables its owner to wear it for a month without having to wind it and retails for $151,000 in platinum.

LONGINES

A SWISS STORY

Longines has been one of the pillars of the Swiss watchmaking industry since it was founded in 1832 in Saint-Imier, Switzerland. Now a subsidiary of the Swatch Group, the company produces around five hundred thousand watches a year. Longines's nonspecialist collections feature thoroughly worthwhile men's and ladies' mechanical pieces.

Master Collection Rétrograde. Automatic watch with 4 retrograde functions and dual time zones.

Longines Weems Second-Setting. Automatic watch with mobile inner dial that can synchronize with radio time signals.

The history of Longines is basically the history of Swiss watchmaking. It all began when Auguste Agassiz opened a watchmaker's shop in Saint-Imier and swiftly achieved an excellent reputation for making classic, solid, but affordable watches. His nephew Ernest Francillon later took over the business and, in 1867, opened a factory named Longines, after the local French patois for the long, narrow meadow on which it was built. With the factory in place, the company tirelessly set to work producing increasingly accurate calibers. Longines also became one of the pioneers in timing athletic events, perfecting the first instrument capable of measuring time to one-fifth of a second in 1878. In 1913 the company released its first single push-button chronograph wristwatch. By the end of the 1920s Longines was so well known that the International Aeronautic Federation asked the company to time Charles Lindbergh's solo transatlantic flight. Longines's association with Lindbergh continued with the 1931 launch of the celebrated hour-angle air navigation watch, designed by Lindbergh to display both the time and the hour angle in degrees and minutes. Five years later the brand released one of the first chronograph wristwatches with a split-time counter and a fly-back function.

Over the years, Longines's experience in timing athletic events gave it the necessary background to develop highly accurate electronic and mechanical watches (such as the Ultra-Chrono and the Ultra-Quartz in the 1960s, and the automatic caliber L990 with calendar function in 1977).

Longines was acquired by the Swatch Group in 1983. After a hiatus the company reentered the market but was weakened by competition from its "big brother," Omega. Since the dawn of the twenty-first century, as Omega has upped its lines' sophistication, Longines has taken its place in the market segment ranging in price from $900 to $16,000. And the watchmaker has managed to climb back to the top, notably by capitalizing on its history (Heritage line, Master Collection) and by launching collections to target young people and/or women, which represent a significant portion of the company's sales.

The Dolce Vita line is emblematic of the Longines style. These rectangular quartz or automatic watches, inspired by a 1930s model, are stylish yet accessible ($995 to $5,000). Turning to more casual watches, in 2007 the brand launched the intelligently

Conquest Ceramic.
Automatic chronograph.

Admiral GMT.
Automatic watch with a second
time zone.

thought-out Longines Sport Collection; this family brings together four lines of sport watches with a contemporary design at fairly affordable prices. The collection offers solid automatic chronographs with the Admiral in steel with ceramic bezels and links for $3,500; some models display a twenty-four-hour time zone at a price of $3,250.

At the same time the company enhanced its selection of mechanical watches. Aside from its famous hour-angle Lindbergh watch, which is available with an automatic movement ($4,500), in 2004 Longines released the Master Collection, a series of entirely mechanical men's watches. The collection includes roughly fifteen models, available in four different cases (from 1.52 inches to 1.87 inches in diameter) with a variety of functions (chronograph, GMT, etc.). Emphasis is placed on finishing (guilloché dials and transparent sapphire backs displaying the movement) and on high-quality calibers (28,800 oscillations per hour). One of the most interesting Master Collection pieces is the automatic chronograph with moon phase, twenty-four-hour display, and day and month display, available for $2,800. Also keep in mind the GMT watch, indicating all twenty-four time zones (using automatic caliber L365, patented by Longines), and especially the Retrograde. Launched in 2007, this automatic model, with movement developed exclusively for Longines by ETA, offers four retrograde functions (day, date, seconds, and second time zone with a twenty-four-hour scale). The 1.73-inch model costs $4,450; $10,500 in rose gold.

At the 2009 Basel Watch Fair, Longines introduced a new column-wheel chronograph movement. Developed with ETA, this excellent caliber (L.688.2) made its debut in the Longines Column-Wheel Chronograph model. With a price that is not expected to exceed $5,100 (a feat for this type of piece), it has the promise of a bright future, especially since the Swatch Group has indicated that it will use the caliber in its other brands—but not at the same price.

RICHARD MILLE

FORMULA ONE MECHANICS

Richard Mille watches are manufactured like racing cars. Although the average price of a tourbillon is $300,000, they are selling like hotcakes.

In 2001, a tourbillon shook up the watch business. With a design as radical as its movement, this revolutionary $135,000 watch set the staid world of *haute horlogerie* afire. Here was a complication watch developed as if it were a car for Formula One racing, a high-stakes arena for which automobile motors and bodies are designed in concert to improve performance and the smallest titanium screws are worth $8 million a pound. At the root of all this turmoil was a simple question from French watchmaker Richard Mille: "I wondered why we continue to make nineteenth-century watches when twenty-first-century technology is available to us."

Mille spared no effort in catapulting one of the oldest and most prestigious of horological complications into the third millennium. Each of his tour de force's 267 parts was dissected, analyzed, and retested before the 20,000 mechanical operations required to construct the watch were begun. The watch's accuracy was improved by 20 percent, while its striking design was conceived for daily wear. Though it does not have a name, an advertising campaign, or, for that matter, a particularly affordable price, the Mille watch is attractive largely to younger collectors—so much so that the brand has difficulties keeping up with demand. Richard Mille produces around 2,300 pieces a year, offering roughly 15 different models, all of which are made of high-tech materials with optimized movements to improve their performance. The carbon-fiber plate fitted in the RM006 to increase the movement's stability is a prime example of this dedication to horological excellence.

In 2005 the company issued the RM009-1 Felipe Massa, developed with the Formula One racer who lent it his name. Though it is the lightest mechanical watch in the world (weighing less than one ounce, without the bracelet), this tourbillon watch can also absorb tremendously heavy vibrations and withstand most shocks. The Felipe Massa was also the first watch to feature an aluminum-lithium plate and an ultralight case made of Alusic (a material previously restricted to high-end aerospace parts). Collectors paid up to $369,300 to snap up one of the twenty-five RM009-1 Felipe Massa limited-edition watches. The RM008 split-time chronograph with a tourbillon is no less impressive. Accuracy and durability are the watchwords of this chronograph, featuring a new and improved split-time counter designed to reduce the movement's power consumption by 50 percent. The RM008 starts at $535,000.

In 2006 Mille launched the RM012: a movement with a very well-built tourbillon with a minimalist structure, characterized by an original tubular construction, which sold

RM012.
Mechanical watch with manual winding and tourbillon.

RM019 Celtic Knot.
Mechanical watch with manual winding and tourbillon.

RM009-1 Felipe Massa.
Mechanical tourbillon watch with Alusic case. Limited edition of 25.

RM025.
Diving tourbillon watch with
automatic movement.

out despite its $493,000 price tag. Two years later the watchmaker revisited the pocket watch by offering an ultracontemporary model that included a tourbillon. In 2009, he courted the female market with the RM019 Celtic Knot. Although the common practice for watchmakers is to simply offer women a smaller version of a man's watch, this watch does not settle for that. In addition to the onyx plate of the movement, the caliber is constructed in the form of a Celtic knot, providing a decorative effect that avoids the pitfall of floweriness. As for its form, this watch incorporates all the specifications— while feminizing them—of Mille models (tonneau case, ergonomic line, visible movement). As for function, its mechanism is impeccable, shock-resistant, and equipped with a variable-inertia tourbillon that improves accuracy ($320,000).

Finally, in 2009 the brand introduced its first round watch: the RM025. This diving chronograph with tourbillon required seven years of development to give a handful of aficionados the privilege of operating a high-tech chronograph 984 feet below sea level. The price of this new toy: around $495,000.

ULYSSE NARDIN

INTELLIGENCE ON THE MOVE

Left for dead less than twenty-five years ago, this Swiss brand is now one of the most innovative companies in the field of timepiece complications. The watch enthusiast delving into the Ulysse Nardin catalog for the first time will discover astronomical watches, minute repeaters with automata, ingenious perpetual calendars, and most impressive of all, the Freak, a wildly unusual watch without hands, dial, or crown.

Since it was founded in Le Locle in 1846, Ulysse Nardin has been awarded 4,300 prizes, including 18 gold medals, for the accuracy of its timekeepers—quite a legacy to live up to. In fact the history of this marine-chronometer specialist (Nardin has sold ten thousand throughout the world) has been far from a walk in the park. Without industrialist Rolf Schnyder's takeover of the company in 1983, for instance, Ulysse Nardin would never have risen from the ashes to which it had been reduced by the devastating sweep of Asian quartz. Schnyder called on the brilliant inventor, astronomer, and science historian Ludwig Oechslin to develop watches that blended complexity and innovation. Sure enough, in 1985 Oechslin made a grand statement with the introduction of the remarkable Astrolabium Galileo Galilei, an astronomical watch set for 104,000 years. This masterpiece measured the altitude and direction of celestial bodies, calculated the seasons and the movements of the zodiac, foretold solar and lunar eclipses, and promptly entered the *Guinness Book of World Records* as one of the most complicated watches in the world. In 1988 Oechslin struck again with the Planetarium Copernicus, featuring a representation of the entire solar system. Three years later he completed his "trilogy of time" with the release of the Tellurium Johannes Kepler. The Tellurium calculated the positions of the sun, the earth, and the moon in relation to one another and to other celestial bodies. With these three celestial watches, Ulysse Nardin successfully reclaimed its position in the galaxy of *haute horlogerie*. Platinum models of all three watches are available as a trio in ninety-nine limited-edition cases, sold for the authentically astronomical price of $150,000. In 2009 the company added a new element to this trio with the Moonstruck. This amazing model simulates the rotation of the moon around the earth, and the apparent movement of the sun around the globe, as well as the respective gravitational effects of the sun and moon on the tides—which are also displayed. Two limited editions of five hundred pieces each have been released ($88,000 for eighteen-karat red gold and $113,000 for platinum).

Today, with production at about twenty thousand watches a year, the company stands out for developing technically original, complex pieces that simply aren't available from any other company. The Nardin collection consists of a vast range of models (including marine chronographs, perpetual calendars, minute repeaters, and dual time zones), at prices ranging from $7,000 to $1,000,000.

Sonata Silicium.
Automatic watch with striking mechanism and second time zone indicator.

Anniversary 160.
Automatic watch with small seconds and large date.

Moonstruck.
Astronomical watch providing moon rotation and the movement of the sun around the earth.

Gengis Khan.
Minute repeater watch with
Westminster carillon striking
work, tourbillon, and jacque-
marts (automated figures).
Limited edition of 30.

GMT Perpetual.
Automatic watch, perpetual
calendar, and second time zone
indicator.

Freak Dimaond Heart.
Mechanical watch with manual
winding and tourbillon karrusel.

Much of the collection focuses on three remarkable Nardin movements: a perpetual calendar movement and the two calibers equipping the Sonata and the Freak, each of which required six years of development. Conceived in 2001, the Freak is a thoroughly aberrant Oechslin creation that tells time through the rotation of its movement. Without hands, dial, or crown, but with a seven-day power reserve, the Freak is a carousel tourbillon equipped with a new silicon escapement that does not require lubrication. In 2005 the Freak was improved with a new double-pulse escapement made of industrial diamonds (the Dual Ulysse escapement), which allows the balance to oscillate 28,800 times per hour. Two years later the watchmaker perfected this piece by fitting it with a new Dual Ulysse (DIAMonSIL) escapement, which combines diamond with silicon. Having sold out worldwide, this culmination of the watchmaker's art is now elusive as it is innovative. At the same time, the brand is capitalizing on its Dual Ulysse by incorporating it into its first basic automatic movement, launched in 2006 to celebrate its 160th anniversary. Fitted with rapid date correction and direct-drive small seconds (to improve accuracy), this COSC–certified watch has been offered in two series of five hundred pieces each (unfortunately sold out).

In 2003 Nardin released the Sonata, an automatic alarm watch featuring an ingenious second time zone that allows the wearer to set the time in one zone without modifying the time in the second zone. Even better, the watch's other functions (alarm, date, etc.) automatically adapt to any change in the time setting (starting at $55,800). In 2008 Nardin released another version, the Sonata Silicium, where the silicon is used both as a decorative element and in certain parts of the movement ($69,000 for rose gold). This intelligent time zone system can now be found on other Ulysse Nardin models, including the GMT +/- Perpetual, which also serves as a perpetual calendar, a complication at which Nardin excels ($47,800 in rose gold). Witness the Perpetual Ludivico, the only automatic perpetual calendar on the market whose calendar functions can all be adjusted forward or backward with a simple turn of the crown. Launched in 1996, the Ludivico is a refreshingly user-friendly complicated timepiece that is priced from $34,800.

More spectacularly, since 2005 the brand has offered the Royal Blue Tourbillon with transparent blue sapphire bridges and plate (from $250,000). And Ulysse Nardin is especially known for minute repeaters featuring automata on their dials. The most impressive of these is undoubtedly the Genghis Khan, a minute repeater with a tourbillon, jacquemarts (automated characters), and Westminster carillon striking work. It lets you enjoy the chiming of the hours in sol, of the minutes in mi, and of the quarter hours on all four gongs, with each gong playing a different note (from 725,000 to 785,000 Swiss francs, or $720,000 to $774,000).

OMEGA

BOTH FEET ON THE GROUND

Seamaster Quantum of Solace.

ProPlof.
Diving watch water resistant to 3,937 feet, automatic movement.

Seamaster Aqua Terra.
Automatic watch with date indicator.

Though they are innovative, sporty, and enjoy a good price-quality ratio, Omega watches don't always get their fair share of success in France. Yet the Swatch Group's nonspecialist watch company is a huge hit everywhere else.

On July 21, 1969, as Buzz Aldrin became the first man to set foot on the moon, the dial of his Speedmaster chronograph read 02h56 GMT. The Speedmaster was an Omega model. Forty years later, what fine Swiss watchmaker would produce an extraterrestrial watch outfitted with a mechanical movement legendary for its reliability and accuracy, all for $2,675? Not a one, save for Omega. Omega, which entered the Swatch Group in 1985, has always striven to make high-quality but affordable watches. In the nineteenth century it was one of the first watch companies to industrialize its production in order to provide precision watches at reasonable prices. Omega's history is rich with spectacular productions. In 1848 Louis Brandt opened his workshop in La Chaux-de-Fonds, Switzerland. A few years later the workshop was moved to Bienne, where it became a manufacture, employed six hundred people and began producing one hundred thousand watches a year. In 1894 the introduction of the Omega pocket caliber 19" (*omega* is a synonym for "accomplishment," like the first and twenty-fourth letters of the Greek alphabet) was such a success that the company adopted its name. The newly minted Omega brand then embarked on a long quest for accuracy, winning several contests and being chosen as official timekeeper of the Olympic Games more than twenty times (including Beijing in 2008 and Vancouver in 2010).

Omega's strategy was perfectly planned: to use assembly-line production to manufacture moderately priced precision watches. As can be expected, Omega watches sold by the millions. In the 1960s the brand became world famous, thanks to two benchmark watches launched simultaneously in 1957, the Seamaster 300 and the Speedmaster. Thirty years later Omega made a technical breakthrough by taking on the mechanical watch escapement, a key component that hadn't been altered in about two hundred years. Devised in cooperation with the great English watchmaker George Daniels, Omega's co-axial escapement allows the movement to run with a bare minimum of lubrication, thereby ensuring greater stability of timekeeping accuracy. Introduced in 1999 after seven years of development, the co-axial escapement now equips 80 percent of Omega mechanical models, or production of more than three hundred thousand movements per year.

The brand is particularly appealing for those desiring to enter the world of mechanical timepieces without going bust, despite that the company has recently increased its prices while increasing the number of precious metal models, limited editions, etc. With

143

Seamaster Planet Ocean.
Automatic chronograph.

Speedmaster Broad Arrow.
Automatic split-second
chronograph.

Hour Vision.
Automatic watch with caliber
visible on the side of the case.

a production of approximately 650,000 to 700,000 pieces a year, Omega is the global leader in sales of watches priced between $3,000 and $4,800. Its collections are vast (more than a thousand models), but uneven in terms of design. The Constellation line, designed at the time by Gérald Genta, a mainstay of the brand's sales, for instance, doesn't exactly break new ground. Despite a makeover in 2009, this collection of ladies' watches, which is highly successful in Asia, is little sought-after in France.

On the other hand, the Seamaster line comes highly recommended and has been one of the company's best sellers since Pierce Brosnan wore a Seamaster as James Bond in *GoldenEye* (1995). Since then the brand has invested in product placement, and for each new Bond film releases a special-edition watch that rarely generates great interest. In the permanent collection, Bond's stylish Seamaster 300 is an excellent diving watch water-resistant to one thousand feet. It is equipped with a COSC–certified automatic movement (caliber Omega 1120 with an ETA 2892 base) and is available for a mere $1,930. Omega's classic line also features a variety of chronograph models, including the elegant Seamaster Aqua Terra, with black dial and brown crocodile bracelet. One may prefer the simplistic all-steel chronometer version launched in 2009 with co-axial escapement ($7,700). In the same family, the $3,450 Seamaster Planet Ocean is water resistant to nearly two thousand feet and features the COSC–certified caliber Omega 2500 with co-axial escapement. One should also mention the renowned PloProf: a professional diving watch launched in the early 1970s that the watchmaker rereleased in 2009. The contemporary version is water resistant to approximately 3,937 feet and has the caliber Omega 8500 with co-axial escapement. It costs $6,700.

The equally legendary Speedmaster line includes the famous Moonwatch, the hand-wound mechanical chronograph (Omega 1861 caliber on a Nouvelle Lemania 1873 base) that was taken for a test run on the moon. The Speedmaster comes in several versions, including a moon phase released in 2003, and column-wheel automatic chronographs, some of which have a split-time counter or GMT function (as in the Speedmaster Broad Arrow, retailing for $12,600). In 2008 Omega profited from its role as official timekeeper of the Beijing Olympic Games by releasing limited-edition watches with dials adorned with the Olympic rings.

Finally, dress-watch aficionados will find what they're looking for in the De Ville line. The remarkable Hour Vision ($14,400) appears here with a partially visible movement on the sides of the case. Introduced in 2007, the watch is fitted with the latest automatic caliber developed in-house, which incorporates co-axial technology. It comes with a GMT function and an annual calendar. Above all it testifies to the determination of Omega to advance in the field of luxury watchmaking.

Moonwatch Apollo 11.
Special edition launched in 2009 to celebrate the 40th
anniversary of the first manned lunar landing.

Shooting for the Moon

The Speedmaster was devised in 1957 to be used in automobile racing. Strangely enough,
its time in the sun wound up taking place on the moon. In 1965, following a rigorous eval-
uation of available models, NASA selected the Omega Speedmaster to be issued to astronauts going on space missions. It was used during the Gemini, Apollo, Skylab, and Shuttle
missions and didn't miss a beat over the course of six moon landings. Most important, the
Speedmaster played a crucial role in helping the crew of the crippled *Apollo 13* return to
earth unharmed. As the only functioning timepiece on board, the Omega Speedmaster
enabled the astronauts to determine the critical moment to fire the rockets and the precise
duration of the motors' combustion to reach and reenter the earth's atmosphere. To this day
the Omega Speedmaster is the only watch to have been worn on the moon. Though enthusiasts may not be able to reach the moon, they can certainly fall back on the Moonwatch
Apollo 11: a special edition launched in 2009 to celebrate the fortieth anniversary of man's
first steps on the moon. On the program are two limited editions: 69 pieces in platinum
(about $102,000) and 7,969 pieces in steel ($6,000). Yet whatever the metal, this is one of
the most beautiful Speedmaster watches that Omega has made.

OFFICINE PANERAI

Luminor Chrono Daylight.
Automatic chronograph with date indicator.

Radiomir Tourbillon GMT.
Automatic watch with manual winding, small seconds, second time zone, and tourbillon.

Luminor 1950.
Single push-button mechanical chronograph with 8-day power reserve, second time zone indicator.

CULT MILITARY WATCHES

Thanks to their oversize cases, extra-resistant models, and long association with the Italian army, Panerai watches have become beloved cult objects—an unusual fate for a brand exclusively designed for military use until 1993.

In Italy hopeless devotees are called Paneristis. In the United States Bill Clinton loves them, while Sylvester Stallone flashes his big Panerai calibers in Hollywood productions. In Asia Paneraimania reigns supreme. Panerai seems to exercise the same power of seduction over the antique watch aficionado and the fashion victim, the professional diver and the jet-setter. With about forty thousand pieces sold per year, Panerai is reaching a level of success close to Rolex's.

The story begins in 1860 in Florence, in the workshop of Guido Panerai & Figlio, a business specializing in optics and precision mechanics. As the official supplier to the Italian navy, Panerai & Figlio prepared precision instruments ranging from chronograph wristwatches to timing devices for exploding mines. Later, with World War II looming on the horizon, the company's collaboration with the navy intensified. In 1936 it began developing a prototype for a diving watch. In 1938 the first watches featuring "Radiomir" (a luminous radium-based substance on the dials' indices) were released with a 1.85-inch cushion case, a wide strap, and an exclusive Rolex movement (caliber 16"). In 1942 a lever system was devised to provide the winding crown with better water resistance. Thanks to this system, Panerai models could descend to 660 feet, a record for the era. In the late 1940s, Panerai developed the Luminor with an Angelus movement (and an eight-day power reserve) and, thanks to the invention of its namesake substance based on tritium instead of radium, an index even more luminous than Radiomir's.

Until 1993 Panerai watches were made exclusively for the army (barely three hundred models were produced for civilians from 1938 to 1992). In 1993 the brand entered civil society with two limited-edition series featuring the Luminor and the Mare Nostrum chronograph (an early 1940s prototype). Between 1993 and 1997, in what is known as its "pre-Vendôme" period (the Richemont group was then called Vendôme), Panerai whet collectors' appetites with a tantalizingly sparse production of 828 watches. In 1997 the Richemont group decided to capitalize on the brand's history by producing formally and technically faithful replicas of its original military models. Over the next five years, Officine Panerai produced more than ninety thousand watches and developed an international stature.

Panerai's current success rests on the brand's knack for transposing characteristics specific to its military watches to the contemporary collection. Aside from a 1.57-inch

Luminor Submersible.
Automatic watch, water resistant to 8,200 feet. Titanium and
steel case.

Radiomir Egiziano.
Mechanical watch with manual
winding.

model designed to accommodate small wrists, Panerai cases have retained their original hefty shapes and dimensions. Dials remain easy to read underwater and in the dark,
and the celebrated crown device continues to provide excellent water resistance. Panerai
movements are based on high-quality Swiss calibers (Valjoux, Jaeger-LeCoultre, etc.) and
are tested in extreme conditions closer to military norms than civilian ones. Panerai
watches are COSC–certified and equipped with an Incabloc shock-absorption system. In
2005 Panerai introduced the first movement entirely conceived and constructed in its
Swiss workshop, the caliber P.2002, featuring three barrels and a vertical eight-day
power reserve, a date display, and dual time zone, in tribute to the Luminor Angelus of
the 1940s. The new movement was released in 2006 in the Radiomir 8 Days GMT. It was
followed by the P.2003, an automatic model with a ten-day power reserve. Panerai then
changed things up with a single push-button chronograph (P.2004) found notably in the
Luminor 1950 Ceramic 8 Days Chrono Monopulsate GMT ($25,600). In 2007 the
Florentine watchmaker released a tourbillon using the P.2005, with its mechanism
visible only on the back of the case. The latest arrival in the family of in-house calibers,
the P.9000, is a solid automatic movement with a GMT function and a power reserve
indicator. In 2009 it appeared memorably in the Luminor 1950 at the (fair) price of
$8,900 for a leather strap.

Although these in-house calibers today represent only an infinitesimal portion of
production, they enable the company to legitimately take its place beside other Swiss
watchmakers, and fuel passion among new collectors ready to spend up to $100,000 to
wear a Panerai with a tourbillon.

In addition to these in-house pieces, Panerai maintains a consistent collection with
steel models that are quite reasonably priced, given their high quality. The Historic line
consists of replicas of the brand's classic models equipped with hand-wound calibers:
the basic Luminor (from $4,400); the Luminor Marina, with small seconds at nine
o'clock, $4,700 to $9,500; and the Radiomir 8 Days, equipped with an eight-day power
reserve ($11,900). The Contemporary line is devoted to self-winding pieces with a variety
of added functions (GMT, power reserve, chronograph, alarm). It includes excellent
diving watches (such as the Luminor Submersible, water resistant to 8,200 feet), robust
chronographs (such as the Luminor Daylight, named after a film starring Sylvester
Stallone, who commissioned it in 1995), and the recent Luminor 1950 chronographs with
split-second or fly-back functions ($11,600 to $17,000). In 2009 true enthusiasts jumped
at the chance to own the rerelease of a model created in 1956 for the Egyptian navy.
This jumbo-sized watch with a case measuring 2.36 inches was released in titanium in
a limited series of five hundred, for $29,000 apiece.

Solid as a Rock

"At −79 Fahrenheit, everything was frozen. The only thing still working was my watch." These are the words of South African adventurer Mike Horn recounting the solo trip he took around the Arctic Circle from August 2002 to October 2004 without a motor. As a sponsor for Horn's "Arktos" expedition, Panerai conceived a watch resistant to temperature variations ranging from −79 to +98 Fahrenheit, magnetic fields (which are particularly strong in the North Pole), shocks, and water. The Panerai Luminor Arktos Amagnetic he wore through 12,242 hours of extreme conditions did not fail him: both the adventurer and the watch made it home safe and sound. In the fall of 2004, Panerai released a limited edition of five hundred of these anti-magnetic automatic pieces with a bezel indicating the four cardinal points.

PARMIGIANI FLEURIER

Bugatti Type 370.
Mechanical watch with a transversal movement, caliber with 10-day autonomy.

Tondagraph.
Chronograph with tourbillon.

Toric Corrector.
Minute repeater watch with perpetual calendar, manual winding movement.

Kalpagraph XXL.
Automatic chronograph.

If Michel Parmigiani's watches are a touch humorless, it's probably to avoid detracting from the imposing technical achievements embodied in their movements. The discreet founder, who is probably the most traditional of contemporary watchmakers, was initially a restorer of *haute horlogerie* pieces. In 1996 he founded his own brand in Fleurier, Switzerland, with funding from the Sandoz Family Foundation. Not satisfied with simply manufacturing the calibers for his own limited production of five thousand pieces a year, in 2003 Parmigiani also set up Vaucher Manufacture Fleurier to produce movements for other leading Swiss watch brands. By dedicating itself to an authentic *haute horlogerie* production—Parmigiani is one of the founders of the Qualité Fleurier certification—Vaucher Manufacture Fleurier is one of the few watch workshops to be directly responsible for all the components of its movements. As of 2005 the company has even produced its own regulating organs (balance wheel and hairspring) and anchor escapements, i.e., the key elements of mechanical calibers.

Thanks to its ten or so brilliantly executed movements (some developed with Renaud & Papi), Parmigiani now appeals to collectors the world over. Its catalog contains two principal lines, the Kalpa and Toric collections. At the top of the pyramid, the Toric Westminster is a small masterpiece of complexity that boasts a carillon minute repeater, a tourbillon, and a dual time zone (starting at $491,200 for rose gold). As for the equally well-designed and user-friendly Toric Corrector, it features a perpetual calendar and a minute repeater, and sells for upward of $321,000. The Tondagraph, launched in 2009, combines a tourbillon and a chronograph in a new case ($200,000).

The more contemporary Kalpa line is characterized by highly ergonomic cases and colored dials. Notably, it includes the Kalpagraph: a handsomely crafted chronograph (caliber PF 334) released in 2007 and offered at a price of $15,900 for steel. Also, the Kalpa Tonda Hémisphères is a very readable automatic model with dual time zone ($18,100 in steel). In a sportier realm, the brand launched in 2008 the Pershing line of nautical watches developed in partnership with the Italian luxury yacht builder of the same name. Notably, it houses the chronograph caliber of Parmigiani.

Car enthusiasts will prefer the Bugatti Type 370 watch. Conceived in 2004 to celebrate the release of Bugatti's latest speedster, the Veyron 16.4, this watch was the first of its kind to be equipped with a horizontal movement that mimics the car's headlights, affording a lateral view of the time (hand-wound caliber 370 with manual windup and ten-day autonomy). This technically masterful, patented beauty is available for $233,900.

PATEK PHILIPPE

THE BEST WATCHMAKER IN THE WORLD

Heures Universelles.
Automatic watch indicating the time in 24 cities around the world.

Nautilus.
Automatic watch with date indicator.

Chronograph 5960P.
Chronograph with fly-back function, annual calendar, and automatic movement.

Quantième Annuel 5146.
Automatic watch with moon phase and annual calendar.

Patek Philippe is to *haute horlogerie* **what Rolex is to sport watches: a living legend. And an exception: since 1839 the company has consistently managed to make good on its vow to "create the most beautiful and precious watches in the world." Whether excessively complex or extremely simple, Patek watches have collectors the world over racing to get in on the action. But the action doesn't come cheap.**

"You'll never really own a Patek Philippe watch. You will simply be its guardian for future generations." Here in the brand's tagline we have the perfect expression of the elusive quality of a watch imbued with a life of its own, of the patrimonial value of an object through which excellence is passed from one generation to the next. In fact, the phrase is an accurate summation of the Patek spirit and the power of attraction the brand exercises on mechanical watchmaking enthusiasts: there's Patek, and then there's all the rest. Founded in 1839 by Adrien de Patek and François Czapek, two Polish refugees in Geneva, the company started off making two hundred finely crafted watches a year. In 1845 Patek met Adrien Philippe, the French inventor of the first keyless winding system. That same year the workshop produced its first minute repeater pocket watch. In 1868, Patek Philippe introduced the first wristwatch in history. The company developed a reputation for the accuracy and quality of its movements, and for the patents it accumulated for innovations such as the perpetual calendar mechanism (1889), the double chronograph (1903), and the Gyromax balance wheel (1949). In 1932 Patek Philippe was acquired by the Stern brothers, whose heirs own the company to this day.

Patek Philippe produces between thirty thousand and thirty-five thousand timepieces a year. From ultraslim models to extracomplicated pieces, the Patek collection covers every style of mechanical timepiece, using about twenty caliber bases (manufactured in-house), for a total of roughly fifty different movements. More than half of the watches produced by the king of Swiss watchmaking feature a variety of complex additional functions or are actual complication watches. It's certainly no coincidence that the three most complicated pocket watches in the world are manufactured by Patek. The Henry Graves, which was completed in 1933 after nine years of development, includes twenty-four complications and remains unchallenged as the most expensive watch in the world (it was auctioned for more than $11 million in 1999). The Caliber 89, released in 1989, set another timepiece record by incorporating thirty-three complications. A Caliber 89 was sold at auction in 2004 for $5.2 million. As for the Star Caliber 2000, released in 2000, it boasted twenty-one complications, including a five-gong striking complication that reproduces all of the Westminster carillon's original melody.

Nicknamed the "Queen of the Auctions," Patek makes virtuoso watches that are

5207.
Minute repeater watch with perpetual calendar and tourbillon.

Celestial.
Astronomic watch showing the movements of the stars and the moon.

Calatrava.
Automatic watch.

mechanical beauties and excellent investments. Witness one of the most complex watches available, the Sky Moon Tourbillon reversible wristwatch released in 2002. The Sky Moon's caliber comprises 686 parts and displays 12 complications, including a sky chart, tourbillon, minute repeater, perpetual calendar, etc.—all for a mere $1.2 million. In 2002 Patek Philippe issued the Celestial, featuring a dial displaying an astonishingly accurate representation of the skies over the Northern Hemisphere, including the positions of the stars and the moon (around $237,500). The following year Patek made a strong impression with the hand-wound 10 Day Tourbillon, featuring a 240-hour power reserve. This COSC–certified mechanical piece with unrivaled autonomy elevates luxury to the point of having a tourbillon cage that does not appear on the dial.

Aside from its celebrated minute repeaters, Patek Philippe produces exquisite perpetual calendars. Its ultrathin automatic repeaters fitted with caliber 240 Q's are benchmarks in the field (starting at $46,300 in yellow gold), especially when they are combined with other complications. The watchmaker is also renowned for its annual calendar, based on a mechanism patented in 1996. This user-friendly calendar watch automatically "recognizes" thirty-day months and thirty-one-day months, and indicates power reserve and moon phase (around $24,600). In 2005 this particularly successful piece was released in a larger case, and then appeared in limited-edition models equipped with a silicon escapement, improving the longevity of the caliber. A major development in 2005 was the release of the slimmest-ever split-seconds chronograph with column wheels (0.21 inches). While all of Patek Philippe's previous chronographs had been conceived with a Nouvelle Lemania movement blank (produced exclusively for Patek), this new chronograph's caliber (CHR 27-525 PS) was made entirely in-house. The initial run only included ten pieces, and only a few are produced each year.

One year later the manufacturer launched the 5960P chronograph, a very contemporary automatic model with column wheel, fly-back function, annual calendar, day/night display, and power reserve ($78,800). The same year Patek Philippe rereleased its cultish Nautilus sport watch, created in 1976. Redesigned in a more contemporary style, it boasts new functions (date counter, moon phase, chronograph) and sustains unprecedented interest among watch enthusiasts ($23,000 on a stainless-steel bracelet).

Fans of more basic timepieces will turn to the Calatrava, which has epitomized the Patek Philippe style since 1932. "Simplicity in its most costly form" consists of a gold or platinum round case, hour and minute indications, an automatic or mechanical movement, and at the very most, seconds and date display. Count on spending about $17,400 for an eighteen-karat yellow-gold case on an alligator strap.

PIAGET

MONSTERS AND MARVELS

Probably the most iconoclastic of Swiss watchmakers, Piaget can jump from creating the slimmest tourbillon in the world to unleashing the most extravagant jewelry watches. The secret of Piaget's success is that it is the only manufacturer to combine authentic mastery of the watchmaker's craft and the jeweler's craft, with a rare touch of daring thrown in.

This company owned by the Richemont group since 1988 is so unusual it can accurately be referred to as the "Piaget exception." Piaget doesn't stop at manufacturing 95 percent of its movements in-house, or even at making all of its cases, bracelets, and crowns. Piaget goes the extra mile and sets up to one million precious stones a year for its jewelry designs. Most important, it is the least Calvinist of Swiss brands, with a taste for creating unique pieces bursting with whimsy and fantasy, yet powered by top-drawer calibers. In other words, Piaget is happy-go-lucky with form and as serious as can be when it comes to content.

Founded in 1874 by Georges Édouard Piaget in La Côte-aux-Fées, the Piaget workshop initially produced timepiece movements for prestigious Swiss brands. In 1943 Piaget registered the company name, began marketing its own watches, and got to work miniaturizing its mechanisms. In 1956 the brand released the famous 9P, an ultrathin hand-wound movement barely 0.08 inches thick. Four years later it introduced the 12P, which, at a thickness of no more than 0.09 inches, was the thinnest automatic caliber in the world. Piaget followed these accomplishments with the 1976 release of the 7P, the thinnest quartz movement of its generation, and, more recently, the 2003 launch of the 600P, the thinnest shaped tourbillon movement in the world.

Ultrathin became the Piaget trademark, providing the brand with an excellent opportunity to break with traditional watch styles. Starting in the 1950s, the Swiss company put its astonishing extravagance on display by designing ring watches and 9P calibers hidden in coins and gold ingots. Piaget also became known for having launched the 1960s fashion for semiprecious stone dials made of onyx, turquoise, coral, and opal mounted on sumptuous cuff bracelets. These pieces are now hotly pursued by collectors.

Today, the "watchmaker's jeweler" produces twenty thousand movements annually. Prices range from about $4,800 for a quartz Possession model to nearly $3 million for one-of-a-kind pieces set with precious stones. Piaget remains one of the few companies to make fine men's and ladies' jewelry watches in the $600,000-and-up range. Particularly favored among Asian collectors, these pricey models are always equipped with one of the manufacturer's twenty in-house calibers. Piaget also excels at producing

Polo Fifty-Five.
Automatic chronograph with fly-back function and second time zone indicator.

Emperador Coussin.
Automatic watch with perpetual calendar.

Emperador Tourbillon.
Mechanical watch, tourbillon at 12 o'clock, 6-hour power reserve indicator.

Polo.
Automatic watch with date
display.

Emperador Coussin.
Automatic watch with perpetual
calendar.

Altiplano.
Ultrathin watch with mechanical
movement amd manual winding.

Polo Tourbillon Venise.
Mechanical watch with a tourbillon placed on the minute
hand.

unusual precious watches featuring turning dials, secret compartments, feathered bracelets, etc. Launched in 1979 and revamped in 2001, the Polo watch is another leading Piaget timepiece. Displaying a perfect blend of luxury and nonchalance, the gold model, with an entirely striated case and bracelet, is the ideal watch for a jet-setter. In 2009 this family grew larger with the addition of the Piaget Polo Forty-Five, a sportier and more contemporary model of this best seller: 1.77-inch titanium cases waterproof to approximately 328 feet incorporate one of two in-house calibers—one three-hand automatic with date ($12,000) and one chronograph with fly-back function and second time zone ($18,000).

The more sober Altiplano line's hand-wound ultrathin watches (caliber 430P, the 9P's successor) are the epitome of Piaget craftsmanship (starting around $10,000 in rose gold). Among Piaget's more complicated pieces, we shouldn't overlook the very beautiful Black Tie Emperador perpetual calendar, launched in 2009 in a cushion-shaped casing. This automatic model with second time zone and retrograde day display is not only very easy to read but also one of the slimmest on the market (about $81,000). Also in the Black Tie line, Piaget released an absolutely sumptuous Emperador Coussin moon phase watch (around $45,000).

The Emperador tourbillon, equipped with a hand-wound caliber 600P that required two years of development, is also very Piaget. Production of this extrathin, extralight flying tourbillon—the forty-two-component cage weighs only 0.2 grams—is limited to about twenty pieces a year. Fans of more expressive pieces will prefer the Polo Tourbillon Relatif, where the tourbillon is placed outside its frame on the minute hand, a piece appearing in limited-edition series, with some models priced just shy of $500,000.

PORSCHE DESIGN

Indicator.
Mechanical chronograph with digital stopwatch display.

P'011.
Automatic chronograph with date display. Steel case and bracelet.

P'6920.
Automatic chronograph with fly-back function.

STREAMLINED CHRONOGRAPHS

Apparently not satisfied with having created the most famous cars of the 1960s, the Porsche 904 and 911, in 1972 Ferdinand Porsche indulged his other passion, watches, by founding Porsche Design in Stuttgart. Two years later he launched his first chronograph, an entirely black model inspired by the dashboard of the 911. This "one-of-a-kind" watch-car hybrid would sell fifty thousand copies. Appropriately, Porsche Design was one of the first watch companies to assert its legitimacy in the field of automobile-inspired timepieces. In the 1980s the company used IWC to manufacture Porsche timepieces, including the first titanium watches on the market, but since it acquired the Swiss Eterna brand in 1995, all Porsche Design models have been conceived in Eterna's workshops. Whether quartz or automatic, steel, titanium, or gold, the company's estimated production of fifteen thousand to twenty thousand watches a year is characterized by ergonomic lines and easily read, uncluttered dials. One of the German brand's leading models is the famous chronograph P'011. Revamped in 2004, the P'011 is fitted with a good automatic movement (Valjoux) and is water resistant to 390 feet (around $3,000). Another interesting piece is the PGR introduced in 2005, a split-second chronograph with a titanium rotor devised to optimize the movement's power (also a Valjoux 7750). Four years later the company is offering another variation: the P'6920 Porsche Design Rattrapante, an automatic chronograph with split-time counter, in a limited edition of two hundred pieces in black PVD-coated titanium ($27,000) and fifty pieces with rose gold ($35,000). Yet Porsche Design's masterstroke—the 2004 introduction of the Indicator—was an entirely unexpected foray into the realm of horological innovation. This unprecedented mechanical watch features the first digital chronometer display, which enables wearers to read elapsed-time measurements at a glance. This eight-hundred-piece movement with a Valjoux 7750 base required three years of development. Porsche Design makes only fifty P'6910 Indicators a year, which goes some way toward explaining the imposing $150,000 price tag.

Eterna Is Back in the Game

Originally founded in Switzerland in 1856, Eterna experienced many travails before its takeover by Porsche Design in 1995. Yet this midrange company, which today produces roughly ten thousand pieces per year, has a few noteworthy innovations to its credit, including, in 1914, the first wristwatch with an alarm function and, in 1948, the Eterna-Matic, the first automatic watch equipped with a ball-bearing system. By the 1970s, after changing hands several times, the brand had reached a state of collapse. Yet the Porsche Design takeover breathed new life into Eterna, which subsequently revamped its collections, notably by rereleasing the KonTiki watch, the model used by explorer Thor Heyerdahl during his 1947 Atlantic crossing on a raft called the *Kon Tiki*. It has been the subject of many variations, such as the KonTiki Chronograph (approximately $3,800) and the KonTiki Diver, released in 2005 and water resistant to 3,280 feet ($9,200). At the same time, the company is emphasizing its classic lines: for example the Madison, with three hands and a manually wound 3501-caliber manufactured in-house ($6,000). In the same vein, the brand is being revived with its own horological craftsmanship. In 2009 the company introduced a new patented caliber, the 3505: a mechanical movement distinguished by its ball bearing–mounted barrel, offering self-lubricating properties and a longer lifespan. It is available in the Madison Three Hands collection for $6,200.

(above) *Madison Three Hands.*
(left) Eterna watch lighter.

RADO

Ceramica.
Quartz chronograph designed by Jasper Morrison.

Ceramica.
Quartz chronograph.

Original Automatic Skeleton.

THE REVIVAL

In the past three years the ceramic-watch specialist has succeeded in its metamorphosis by repositioning its collections within the realm of design. Alongside the new line designed by Jasper Morrison, the brand is now offering more desirable and contemporary models.

There was the worst—let's not forget the extreme hideousness of those ceramic watches decorated with Maori tattoo designs—but today there should only be the best. Rado was not content simply with being the first company to launch a ceramic model (in 1986); being loved by the Chinese, Americans, and Germans; and producing between four hundred thousand and five hundred thousand watches per year. It got the idea to reconquer the European markets known for luxury (i.e., France and Italy), where the pragmatic discourse of this Swatch Group brand boasting about its watches' hardness and scratchproof qualities fell on deaf ears.

For more than fifty years the obsession of this company—established in Longeau, Switzerland, in 1917, and producing under the Rado name since 1957—was to create a watch that used the most resistant materials available. The first opus arrived in 1962: the DiaStar, with a case manufactured in hard metal (a titanium and tungsten-carbide alloy) and equipped with a sapphire-crystal glass that ensured it the then-envied title "first scratchproof watch in the world." It was a huge success: three million DiaStar pieces have been sold since then. In the 1980s, still on a quest for indestructible materials, Rado created the high-tech ceramic watch, employing a material that had already proven itself in the aeronautical industry by serving as a heat shield for space shuttles during their return to the earth's atmosphere. Rado's idea did not explode in flight. The first model, the Rado Integral, equipped with a ceramic strap, appeared in 1986 and now range from $3,000 to $20,000 for a style fully encrusted with pave diamonds. Four years later the brand launched the Ceramica, which went all-in with this new material by incorporating it into a high-tech black cuff watch. In the 1990s Rado became the expert of this tireless scratchproof ceramic watch, which is now priced between $2,800 and $20,000 (for the diamond-encrusted variety).

Yet the company's single-minded focus on the technical nature of the product ended up killing the dream. After changing course in the first decade of twenty-first century, Rado repositioned itself within the area of design by curtailing the number of its collections, which decreased from 800 to 270 models. The majority of the watches are quartz, with an average price of $2,000 to $4,000. The flagship pieces, such as the DiaStar and the Ceramica, have been restyled in more modern proportions and stripped of their past embellishments, as, for example, the latest Ceramica XL Jubilé models—

Esenza.
Quartz watch.

R5.5.
Quartz chronograph designed
by Jasper Morrison.

Ceramica XL.
Cuff watch, dial set, quartz
movement.

in pure black monochrome contrasted with a green or pink "halo" of light, according to the tint of the dial's glass ($20,000 with pavé diamonds); or the Esenza, with a case in perfectly flat black with an oval shape that is given heft by the presence of the gold edge contour ($2,000).

At the same time the brand has recently enlisted the services of famed designer Jasper Morrison. After signing for a limited series of fifty pieces of the Ceramica chronograph in 2007 that were snapped up immediately, he unveiled a new opus in 2009 that promised to symbolize the renaissance of the brand. Morrison is said to have designed it "without visual pollution." He says, "A watch must be an intelligent response to a need of consumers." This new Rado, available for between $2,300 and $2,800, should speak to them.

ROLEX

Submariner Date.
Automatic diving watch with date indicator, water resistant to 985 feet.

Milgauss.
Automatic watch with magnetic field resistance.

Cosmograph Daytona Leopard.
Automatic chronograph. Diamond markers and bezel set with yellow sapphires.

Oyster Perpetual Day-Date.
Automatic watch with day of the week and date indicator. Gray gold case and bracelet.

A ROLEX OR NOTHING AT ALL

Today its sales average seven hundred thousand pieces a year. The global leader in luxury timepieces originally built its reputation on its celebrated waterproof Oyster case, which was launched in 1926, and on its no-less-famous Perpetual Rotor automatic movement, introduced in 1931. Since then Rolex has transcended fashion with consistently accurate, reliable models.

Watchmaking insiders typically explain the success of Rolex—whose total number of watches in circulation is estimated at more than twenty million—by saying, "Rolex is successful because it's Rolex!" New brands rise and fall, fashions come and go, but Rolex remains. Immutable, always the same, resolutely impervious to the trend for complicated movements and to the boundless quest for technical prowess. It cares not a whit about the desperate battles being waged by international collectors to get hold of a Daytona Paul Newman or a vintage Submariner, and it firmly refuses to release the most trivial financial data. In fact, it is said that the Rolex Company has become a foundation that no longer even needs to sell its watches. In other words, Rolex is just like its watchcases: hermetically sealed off from the outside world. Rolex's splendid isolation is the secret of its power.

The Swiss company's global success story begins in 1905 in London, with the founding by Hans Wildorf, a Bavarian, of a company specialized in the distribution of timepieces. Three years later Wildorf coined the name Rolex. In 1910 he obtained the first Swiss chronometer certification for a wristwatch. In the 1920s Rolex took its growing reputation for precision and high quality and moved to Geneva. In 1926 it released the first waterproof watch, the Oyster. It was indeed "tight as an oyster"—in 1927 this particular "oyster" made it across the English Channel on British swimmer Mercedes Gleitze's wrist without missing a beat. Four years later Rolex perfected its invention by developing and patenting the Rotor Perpetual, the first automatic movement with a rotor, and a precursor to today's automatic watches. The foundations of the Rolex myth were in place. Year by year, decade by decade, the myth was built up, with one innovation after another: the Datejust, the first watch of its type to display the date (1945); the Submariner, the first watch water resistant to 330 feet (1953); the GMT-Master II, with two time zones; the Day-Date, the first watch to spell out the day of the week (1956); the Cosmograph Daytona (1963), a chronograph that developed a cult following once it was spotted on race-car driver Gianni Agnelli's wrist in 1985; and the Sea-Dweller, water resistant to 2,130 feet, used by divers working for the deep-sea engineering company Comex (1967).

Today's Rolexes retain the attributes that have made the company's watches best sellers for many decades. In the Rolex family there are 170 models available in 3,200 combinations. There are no revolutions, just subtle evolutions: one model may inherit a slightly

Sea-Dweller Deepsea.
Diving watch, water resistant
to 12,800 feet, automatic
movement.

Yacht-Master II.
Regatta chronograph with
countdown function.

Lady Oyster Perpetual.
Automatic watch.

DateJust II.
Automatic watch with date
display at 3 o'clock.

more rounded case, another a bracelet with solid links or new clasps, yet another might have its hands and markers enlarged in order to enhance legibility. Over the past fifteen years the persistence with which Rolex has worked at improving its models has finally led it to begin manufacturing its own components. Producing everything from dials to bracelets and from crowns to spiral balances, Rolex has become a wholly independent manufacturer.

Experts believe Rolex currently produces between seven hundred thousand and eight hundred thousand watches a year. Rolex also takes the prize for producing the highest number of watches certified by the COSC. Accuracy is certainly no stranger to Rolex's international success. Anecdotes relating a Rolex's miraculous return to life after spending years trapped under the ice on Mount Everest or deep under the seas are too numerous to count, and frequently even turn out to be true. There is no shortage of reasons to succumb to the temptation of owning a Rolex. These sport watches will never go out of fashion and will always retain their cachet. They appreciate in value at the speed of light, are extraordinarily reliable, and, given their high quality, quite reasonably priced. In the Oyster line of automatic watches, you can buy into the myth starting at $4,000 for a steel mini Oyster Perpetual, just over an inch wide and water resistant to 330 feet. The famous Datejust, with date display at three o'clock and a "Cyclope" magnifying glass, starts at $5,050 for the solid steel model, and about $5,900 when it includes the famous steel-and-gold "Rolesor" bracelet. In 2009, it reappeared with a more ample case. As a bonus this Datejust II runs on the new caliber 3136 developed by Rolex, distinguished by its resistance to shocks and magnetic fields by virtue of its Parachrom spiral and its Paraflex system ($7,525 to $11,175). Following the same principle, the brand launched the Day-Date II, with a 1.61-inch case and the same automatic caliber, which starts at $27,650.

Another choice piece, the Submariner Date, is water resistant to 985 feet and, thanks to its unidirectional green bezel and its black dial, undoubtedly one of the most beautiful diving watches on the market (from $6,000). In 2008 it appeared with a blue ceramic bezel and the famous in-house automatic movement. That same year Rolex launched the all-new Sea Dweller: the Deepsea, water resistant to approximately 12,795 feet, a record ($9,250). Another noteworthy watch in the maritime realm is the Yacht-Master II, released in 2007. It is a regatta chronograph distinguished by its countdown feature, programmable from the bezel and linked to the movement ($33,650 to $37,150). As for the Cosmograph Daytona, which has been fitted with the new 4130 caliber manufactured by Rolex since 2000 (it previously contained an El Primero movement made by Zenith), it has aroused such enthusiasm that you'll have to wait of several months to get one and lay out a minimum of $9,925 (for the steel model) before you can strap it to your wrist. The same goes for the Milgauss introduced in 2007 and inspired by a 1950s model. Its name is the contraction of the French words *mille* (thousand) and *gauss*, the unit of measurement of magnetic fields. Its automatic movement— again a fully in-house caliber—perfectly resists electromagnetic waves (around $6,200).

SEIKO

AN OBSESSION WITH PRECISION

Roughly 6,200 miles from Switzerland, in the mountains of the prefecture of Nagano, Japan, Seiko has built a watchmaking industry from scratch with the sole mission of putting horological accuracy within reach of its compatriots. As a bonus, the company has also introduced unique calibers like the Spring Drive, which allows time to glide by smoothly on the dial.

Roughly 6,200 miles from Switzerland, in the mountains of the prefecture of Nagano, Japan, Seiko has built a watchmaking industry from scratch with the sole mission of putting horological accuracy within reach of its compatriots. As a bonus, the company has also introduced unique calibers like the Spring Drive, which allows time to glide by smoothly on the dial.

Although the quest to create high-performance watches is common to all watchmakers, at Seiko the pursuit is quasi-obsessive. In Japanese *seiko* means "precision." And it is no accident that this company, founded in 1881 in Tokyo by Kintaro Hattori, was the first in the world to launch a quartz watch, in 1969. The goal was twofold: to attain the most absolute precision and to make it available to everyone. That took ten years. "We produce watches but not electronic components," a spokesperson at the company headquarters affirmed. "We therefore had to develop them ourselves. We did not know the rules, we did not have the specifications. That is what has made us strong: being so far from Switzerland has enabled us to create our own horological industry from the ground up."

Forty years later the Japanese giant manufactures 347 million quartz movements and assembles 13 million watches per year. It is known for combining traditional horological craftsmanship with a very specialized technology in fluid collections, not all of which are distributed in Europe. Its strong suit is also offering truly innovative watches, some of which have no equivalent on the market, at prices that stand up to any competition. By way of example is the Kinetic: introduced in 1988, it was the first quartz watch without a battery that, like an automatic model, used the movements of the wrist (which it transforms into electricity) to recharge itself. This process is visible on the Kinetic Direct Drive, which displays the energy of the wearer as it accumulates in the power reserve placed on the dial.

Since then this ecofriendly caliber has outfitted numerous models of the brand (Arctura, Sportura, Premier, etc.) and has been combined with various functions (chronograph, perpetual calendar, retrograde day display, etc.), one of which is a beautiful moon phase launched at the Basel Watch Fair in 2009 (approximately $1,700).

Next to the Kinetic the spearhead of Seiko is, without any doubt, the Spring Drive caliber. Twenty-eight years of research and development and six hundred prototypes were necessary to create this phenomenal movement, which was released in 2005. This piece is constructed as a mechanical watch with springs and gear trains, and it enjoys the luxury of functioning without the mainstay of traditional Swiss horology, the escapement. Instead Seiko

Ananta.
Automatic watch with retrograde day and date.

Ananta.
Spring Drive chronograph.

Sportura Kinetic Direct Drive.
Quartz watch without battery, power reserve indicator.

Spring Drive SNR017.
Spring Drive movement with moon phase display.

has replaced the escapement with a tri-synchro regulator (simultaneously electric, electronic, and magnetic) that offers the precision of quartz by varying only by one second per day. And as there is no escapement, the hands no longer jump on the dial; rather, they glide along in silence. Time is no longer fragmented; it flows naturally. This jewel by Seiko is a good alternative to luxury Swiss watches. With a price range starting in the neighborhood of $4,300, this Spring Drive collection, with a very classic look, offers several models, including a column-wheel chronograph and a GMT, both highly regarded.

The Spring Drive caliber can also be found in the Ananta line, introduced at the 2009 Basel Watch Fair. It had been a long time since Seiko had launched such a well-executed line. As much in function as in form, Ananta combines all the strong points of the Japanese watchmaker's identity: a design both powerful and sophisticated in its finishing, and first-rate components manufactured entirely in-house. Five watches are offered in this line: two are equipped with the Spring Drive technology (the chronograph and the GMT) and three have automatic calibers (a chronograph, a double retrograde, and a three-hand with day and date). The prices are incredible considering the quality of the models: from $2,100 to $6,400.

The Sound of Japan

Introduced in 2006, the Credor Spring Drive Sonnerie is a horological curiosity that need not be envious of its Swiss counterparts. Each is priced at more than $100,000, and the watchmakers of the Suwa workshop make only five per year. This watch with *sonnerie* mechanism reproduces the sound of the Orin bell, the traditional prayer bell of the Buddhists. To faithfully imitate the pure resonance of this sound and its subsequent ebb, Seiko incorporated a tiny bell into the watch's case, miniaturized by a specialist in the field. Small engravings on the front form the shape of a campanula (or bellflower), a very popular flower in Japan. The open areas between the bridges evoke the currents of a river, while the mechanism's tiny rubies vary in size to depict a field of flowers. Precision has become one with aesthetic, and Seiko has possibly invented the first Buddhist watch.

Credor Spring Drive. With fly-back function.

SWATCH

Swatch Once Again.
Quartz watch.

Irony Chronograph.
Quartz chronograph.

Launched in 1983 to fend off cheaper quartz models from Asia, Swatch, the first Swiss watch made of plastic, met with phenomenal success. Nearly thirty years later, more than 400 million Swatches have been sold around the world, but the company's concept of a lighthearted, accessible timepiece is now being encroached on by fashion brands.

In the words of Nicolas G. Hayek, chairman of the Swatch Group, "This watch is my talisman. The Swatch allowed me to save the Swiss watch industry and keep my factories and use them for innovation." Flashback: in the late 1970s the Swiss watch business was being brought to its knees by the rise of Asian quartz and supplanted on the global market by the industry in Hong Kong and Japan. Deeply rooted in the production of traditional mechanical movements, the most prestigious timepiece manufacturers found themselves up for sale. Swiss banks turned to Hayek, an industrial restructuring consultant, for help. Hayek decided to try and beat the Asian watch industry with a European-style plastic quartz watch produced in Switzerland. His plan was inspired by the Delirium Tremens, the thinnest gold watch in the world (0.04 inches thick), created by ETA in 1979. The Delirium Tremens's secret was a radically reduced number of components. Three years later the Delirium Vulgare saw the light of day, with fifty-one components, a plastic case and strap, and a production cost of eight Swiss francs. On March 1, 1983, the first black model with a white dial was unveiled in Zurich, with a new name formed of a contraction of the words Swiss and watch: Swatch. Chic yet truly affordable, offbeat, and creative, the Swatch ushered in a new era for the Swiss watch industry, transforming the watch into a fashion accessory while offering a level of quality (accuracy, water resistance, shock resistance) previously restricted to far more expensive models. Swatch's success was global: three million watches were sold in 1984, and twice that in 1985. Meanwhile, Hayek refined his marketing by asking artists to design limited-edition Swatches. In 1985 Kiki Picasso came up with her own Swatch, and each of the 140 models was given to a privileged trendsetter. The Kiki Picasso was followed by the Keith Haring, the Mimmo Paladino, the Sam Francis, etc., unleashing an unprecedented speculative frenzy. By the late 1980s some models of the plastic watch, which was then available in stores for less than $55, were being auctioned for more than $36,000. In time, Swatch opened its collections to chronographs (1990), automatic movements (1991), music (with the MusiCall, 1993), steel (the Irony, 1994), ski slopes (the Access, 1995, sold with lift passes), ultrathin models (the Skin, 1997).

Although the brand today produces between eleven million and fifteen million timepieces per year and has the second-largest sales figures in the Swatch Group behind

Irony Timeless.
Automatic skeleton watch.

Swatchtable.
Vegetable-shaped quartz
watch launched in 1991.
Limited edition.

Chrono Plastic Snow Pass.
Quartz chronograph.

Omega, it would seem that "Swatchmania" has run out of steam. Speculation has collapsed—pieces sold at the latest Swatch auctions failed to reach estimated prices. What's more, the giant of the plastic watch has been severely undermined by the numerous other brands entering the same market. Nevertheless, Swatch remains the benchmark for reasonably priced, fashionable watches. With an average price of $95 and continually expanding lines (three hundred new models added annually) rich in both style and function, the company has not strayed from the principle stated by its founder: "To make a Swiss watch in plastic of high quality at a low cost, that is both provocative and fanciful, and worn by kings and paupers alike."

Each prospective buyer will therefore find a piece to suit. There is the simply designed Swatch Original, with a black case, white dial, three hands, and date ($50); the attention-getting Irony Golden Chest chronograph in PVD-coated steel ($200); sporty models equipped with altimeters or that are water resistant to 656 feet; or the Fine Engine with Swatch Snowpass technology, which incorporates a ski pass for ski resorts ($120). With models like these, everyone can enjoy wearing one every day.

Swatch by Manish Arora.
Quartz watch.

Skin.
Extrathin watch with quartz
movement.

TAG HEUER

ON THE CUTTING EDGE OF ACCURACY

In the span of a few years TAG Heuer has created a new standard in sport watches by producing chronographs accurate to tenths, hundredths, and even thousandths of a second, and by maintaining an edgy design style fueled by innovative concepts.

In 2005 TAG Heuer made headlines by introducing the Caliber 360, the first mechanical chronograph accurate to 1/1,000th of a second. Given that 90 percent of chronographs are quartz and only measure time to a tenth of a second, the Caliber 360 heralded a major accomplishment. Of course this wasn't the first time TAG Heuer had stood out from the crowd: in 2002 TAG Heuer garnered much attention with the launch of the Microtimer, the only digital watch on the market accurate to 1/1,000th of a second. As can be surmised from the previous sentences, this Swiss brand bought by LVMH in 1999 is characterized by its obsession with chronometric accuracy. With production of around five hundred thousand watches a year, TAG Heuer ranks fourth among international upmarket sport watch manufacturers. And though it is one of the most dynamic brands on the market, it has never deviated from the strategy initially outlined by company founder Edouard Heuer in 1860 in the Swiss Jura: to offer the most accurate, reliable timepieces possible.

TAG Heuer initially made a name for itself in the world of high-level athletic competitions by developing a wide variety of chronometry systems. Along with being one of the first to mass-produce pocket chronographs (1882), Heuer introduced the oscillating pinion (1887), still used in most mechanical chronographs, and conceived the Mikrograph (1916), the first sport timer to measure time to 1/100th of a second. In 1966 this drive for accuracy led the company to revolutionize the history of chronometry with the introduction of the Microtimer, a miniature electronic instrument accurate to 1/1,000th of a second. Three years later Heuer made sport-watch history with the release of the Chronomatic Calibre 11. Developed in collaboration with Büren and Breitling, and equipped with an 11 caliber and microrotor, the Chronomatic was the first automatic chronograph movement. Later in 1969 Heuer issued the Monaco, the first chronograph with a square, water-resistant case, worn by Steve McQueen in the car-racing film *Le Mans*.

In 1985 the TAG Group (TAG stands for Technique d'Avant-Garde), the owner of the McLaren Formula One racing stable, acquired Heuer and ushered the company into the media spotlight by creating high-concept advertising campaigns, hiring celebrity-brand ambassadors/athletes, and establishing it as the official timekeeper of Formula One Grand Prix races and the Alpine Ski World Cup. TAG provided Heuer with powerful marketing for its sport watches (the S/el, now known as Link, and Kirium lines, for instance), which in turn made their mark on timepiece design with their sleek, ergonomic looks.

Monaco Classic Chronograph.
Automatic chronograph.

Aquaracer 500.
Diving watch water resistant to 1,640 feet.

Calibre 360.
Chronograph accurate to 1/10th of a second, automatic movement. Steel case.

Link Calibre S.
Electromechanical chronograph, accurate to within 1/100th of a second.

GRAND Carrera.
Automatic chronograph with time indicator to 1/10th of a second.

Since it was purchased by LVMH, TAG Heuer has renewed its entire range of watches and driven its reasonably priced models into every segment of the sport watch market. Prices in the line range from less than $1,000 (Formula One) to the neighborhood of $7,000 (TAG Heuer GRAND Carrera). Most of its quartz and mechanical movements are based on those by ETA, Valjoux, Zenith (for the 36 caliber), or Seiko, which conceived the calibre 1887, an automatic chronograph presented by TAG Heuer in December 2009.

Among the more innovative pieces, the caliber S is an electromechanical movement that measures and displays times down to 1/100th of a second. These caliber S chronographs (in the Aquaracer and Link lines) offer unequaled readability, as they provide, in chronograph mode, time measurements without relying on subdials (starting around $2,300 for a Link chronograph). The Calibre 360, introduced at the 2005 Basel Watch Fair, is another landmark model. Three years of work went into developing this mechanical chronograph, accurate to 1/100th of a second. The Calibre 360 combines two individual mechanical movements controlled by a single crown. Aside from the 360's classic automatic movement, which alternates 28,800 times per hour, the chronograph function is driven by another mechanism alternating 360,000 times per hour. It is therefore ten times more accurate than the most accurate wrist chronograph currently available. It has appeared in a limited series, the Carrera Calibre 360, which won an award at the Grand Prix d'Horlogerie de Genève in 2006.

Equally unique is the Caliber 36 RS Caliper Concept Chronograph. Launched in 2008, in the GRAND Carrera line, this automatic movement offers instant readability of times measured, thanks to a fixed indicator and rotating disks that replace traditional hands. This model, accurate to 1/10th of a second, has won several awards. It costs $12,400.

In a more classic realm, in 2009 the brand gave a makeover to the Aquaracer 500 line of automatic diving watches water resistant to approximately 984 feet. They are very fine models at $1,400. The year 2009 also marked the fortieth anniversary of the Monaco. Aside from limited editions, the brand launched a new Classic line, automatic chronographs (caliber 12) that are being revived with the watch's original design from 1969 ($4,500).

Monaco V4.

The Monaco V4

Introduced in 2004 at the Basel Watch Fair, this "horological UFO" has caused a sensation. The concept, conceived with the great Swiss watchmaker Philippe Dufour, is new to say the least: to create the first automatic mechanical movement that functions without a gear train! In this watch, the energy is transferred no longer by traditional gear wheels but by belts cut from high-tech materials that are more shock resistant. Second innovation: the replacement of traditional rubies by a ceramic ball-bearing system. Third feat: the form of the oscillating mass—linear, not round, which allows for a slimmer movement. The watch also features four barrels and a power reserve of seventy days.

After numerous refinements, the Monaco V4 finally saw the light of day in September 2009— in a limited edition of 150 pieces that scarcely resemble the initial prototype.

TISSOT

THE HAPPY MEDIUM

This pivotal Swatch Group brand produces more than two million watches a year. Tissot supplies nonspecialist collections and midrange markets with timepieces that may be innovative but manage to be consistently reassuring.

In the family of traditional Swiss timepiece brands, Tissot could be the provincial uncle: modest, reliable, yet up-to-date on modern technologies. While some companies lose themselves in timepiece complications, flaunt their achievements, and drive prices sky high with "world premieres," Tissot stays on course by producing reasonably priced (between $180 and $960), well-crafted watches that happen to fly off the shelves. In 2009 the brand sold 2.3 million pieces. Tissot, which has belonged to the Swatch Group since 1985, now produces more watches than any of the group's classic brands.

Founded in 1853 in Le Locle, Switzerland, by Charles-Édouard Tissot and his son, Charles-Émile, the company initially conceived robust, user-friendly watches. Before long it invented a dual time zone fob watch, then conquered the Russian market in 1904 with the Watch of the Czars military watch. In 1933 Tissot launched the first antimagnetic watch. In 1953 it released the twenty-four time zone Navigator. Eighteen years later the company unveiled the Idea 2001, the first watch equipped with a mechanical movement made of plastic and therefore free of the wear and tear and lubrication problems inherent in a classic mechanism. Sadly, this invention would be obscured by the appearance of quartz. Yet Tissot was quick to bounce back with its own take. In 1978 it released a multifunction quartz chronograph featuring analog and numeric displays, and in 1996 it equipped its models with ETA's Autoquartz movement, which combines the accuracy of quartz with an automatic winding mechanism.

Though it now uses quartz in the majority of its models, Tissot has recently invested several million euros to develop with the Swiss movement company ETA (which also belongs to the Swatch Group) a new automatic caliber. Unveiled at the 2009 Basel Watch Fair, the Co1.211 offers a price-quality ratio that stands up to any competition, and the brand expects to begin producing at least a hundred thousand per year. The new movement can be found in the Tissot Couturier, a rather simple automatic chronograph sold for $450. At the same time, the manufacturer remains true to its "traditionally innovative" motto. Its varied, nearly overabundant range of watches covers all the major timepiece styles—sport, fashion, and classic—with comfortable, frequently inventive products. A prime example is the 2000 T-Touch: this multifunctional model has become one of Tissot's best sellers, with more than one million sold. This quartz watch, which comes in several versions, features a pressure-sensitive face that alternately displays a chronograph, altimeter, thermometer, barometer, compass, and alarm, all at

Tissot Couturier.
Automatic chronograph.

T-Sport.
Automatic chronograph.

T-Touch.
Quartz watch with multifunction tactile dial.

T-Race Moto GP2009.
Automatic chronograph.

the touch of a finger. As for sport watches, the brand is known for the T-Race line of large chronographs inspired by the world of motorcycles, and for the PRS516 collection. The PRS516 features an excellent self-wound reinterpretation of a model initially released in 1966, including a movement visible through the back of the case and a perforated leather strap, available for $1,450.

Tissot is also the Swatch Group's biggest manufacturer of gold watches, and one of the few Swatch companies to include pocket watches in its collections. Tissot's rather well-conceived ladies' watches account for 45 percent of its sales.

For the last few years Tissot has been reissuing classic models through its Heritage line. Each year this line offers retro designs equipped with automatic movements at— what else?—affordable prices.

VACHERON CONSTANTIN

CRAFTING BEAUTY

Patrimony Day-Date Rétrogrades. Automatic watch with retrograde day and date.

Quai de l'Ile. Personalizable automatic watch with the date and day of the week.

Les Metiers d'Art. Limited edition of watches with dials displaying masks from the Barbier-Muller collection.

It has taken the oldest watch manufacturer in the world more than two and a half centuries of hard work, the production of exceptional *haute horlogerie* timepieces, and a major auction in 2005 to finally ascend to the elevated rank it rightfully deserves.

The brand's directors have stated that "though we exist in a prestigious world, it is important for us to stay humble, and to strictly adhere to our ethic"—an unusual approach in a field where arrogance is legion. Indeed, Vacheron Constantin, which was bought by the Richemont group in 1996, enjoys a special place in contemporary horology: its technical expertise goes hand in hand with its meticulous quest for beauty. To this end the brand imbues every step that goes into crafting a watch with the legacy of its heritage. Ethic and beauty are the bywords of the company, whose production is limited to fewer than twenty thousand pieces per year.

The notion of harmonizing a watch's style with its interior workings was born in 1755, when Jean-Marc Vacheron opened his Geneva *cabinotier* workshop (*cabinotier* was the name given to Geneva's master clockmakers). Vacheron's magnificent watches were pocket pieces with fusee movements and verge escapements engraved with acanthus leaves. In 1819 the Vacheron business entered into a partnership with François Constantin, an indefatigable traveler who roved the world selling finely worked watches that displayed a perfect marriage of technique and aesthetics. Constantin came up with the motto "Do better if possible, which is always possible." In 1839 the mechanical genius Georges-Auguste Leschot took Constantin at his word and revolutionized production with the invention of a machine that allowed for watch parts to be interchangeable. Vacheron Constantin became the first company to mechanize its production, thereby providing its movements with an incomparable level of precision.

Yet Vacheron Constantin has never turned its back on human craftsmanship. To this day each piece is elaborated and finished by hand, and more than 75 percent of the watches to come out of the Vacheron Constantin workshop bear the Poinçon de Genève, the mark of the highest level of watchmaking craft. The ultrathin watches fitted with the .04-inch-high caliber VC, manufactured in the 1950s and 1960s, have become archetypes of their kind, as have the watches with finely enameled dials in the Métiers d'Art series. The brand offers a clean, sophisticated aesthetic in its finishing (even the most minute pieces have been discreetly decorated with *côtes de Genève*).

Truly representative of the brand, the Patrimony line undoubtedly offers the most elegant city watches available. The Patrimony Traditionnelle (1.5 inches) with small seconds boasts a three-day power reserve thanks to a new movement, the 4400, developed in-house in 2009 ($18,900 in rose gold). In addition to a chronograph (caliber

Patrimony Traditionnelle.
Mechanical watch with manual
winding and small seconds.

Malte Tourbillon Régulateur.
Regulator watch with tourbillon.

Cabinotiers.
Skeleton watch with minute
repeater, mechanical movement,
and manual winding.

11421 with a Lemania base) and a perpetual calendar, in 2008 the brand launched a chic automatic model in platinum with retrograde date and day ($87,500). Vacheron Constantin is also known for its shaped pieces, such as the Toledo 1952 and the Historiques American 1921, but especially the Malte: a flagship line with tonneau cases that house various movements (chronograph, perpetual calendar, dual time zone, etc.), some of which are high voltage, such as the very well-balanced Malte Tourbillon Regulator (with a minute hand separate from the hour hand), available for $201,000.

Another of the Vacheron workshop's specialties is its skeleton watches, in which the case is emptied of 70 percent of the movement and the rest is engraved by hand. In the high-complications workshop, Vacheron Constantin's watchmakers spend two thousand hours crafting a single skeleton minute repeater. The time invested in these precious models is reflected in their retail value: they are sold for around $631,000. And due to the laborious, complex process required to obtain the crystalline timbre of their chime, only ten of the skeleton minute repeaters are released each year. (One essential step, for instance, is to bathe the repeater's components in horse urine for several hours.) Vacheron Constantin also produces ten skeleton tourbillons a year, which also require an equal amount of work.

In 2008, Vacheron Constantin branched out into more contemporary pieces. For example, there's the Quai de l'Ile Personalised transparent watch, with a dial made of a completely customizable polymer film that leaves exposed the beauty of the in-house calibers. Launched in two models, an automatic with date and a perpetual calendar with the day of the week and the date (from $34,900 to $41,600), this piece is representative of the brand, whose motto could easily be Lao-Tzu's: "Enlighten without blinding."

An Anniversary Anthology

To celebrate its 250th anniversary in 2005, the company released five exceptional new collections. The Esprit des Cabinotiers is an intriguing clock symbolizing the art of the watchmaker's craft: a rose-gold sphere, engraved by hand, unfolds like the petals of a flower to reveal a finely crafted dial displaying moon phases, equation of time, a second time zone, and a perpetual calendar, along with an eight-day power reserve and a thermometer. A collector bought this unique piece for just over 2.2 million Swiss francs.

Another incredible piece is the Tour de l'Ile, in a limited edition of seven. With sixteen complications divided between its two faces, this masterpiece has laid claim to the distinction of being the most complicated wristwatch in the world. Ten thousand hours of research and development, 834 components housed in a 1.85-inch case and a caliber awarded the Poinçon de Genève, all add up to a watch costing more than $1.5 million.

Another one of Vacheron Constantin's world premieres is the Saint-Gervais Grandes Complications, a four-barrel mechanical watch with a 250-hour power reserve, a tourbillon, and a perpetual calendar. Fifty-five platinum pieces have been released, at a price of $380,000 each.

Vacheron Constantin also issued twelve Métiers d'Art collectors' boxes containing four automatic watches with enameled dials, each representing one of the four seasons ($340,000 for the set). Finally, the Jubilé 1755 series, limited to 1755 pieces ($27,000 in rose gold), is fitted with the Vacheron workshop's new automatic movement, the caliber 2475. With a frequency of 28,800 vibrations per hour and a 42-hour power reserve, the Jubilé 1755 combines reliable accuracy with a particularly beautiful mechanism.

VAN CLEEF & ARPELS

Midnight in Paris.
Mechanical watch displaying the constellations.

Lady Arpels Centenaire.
Mechanical watch displaying the seasons.

Alhambra Vintage.
Quartz watch.

TIMELY JEWELS

Although watchmaking is not currently central to the jeweler's strategy, it is developing more and more. In three years Van Cleef & Arpels—which, according to our estimates, produces between three thousand and five thousand pieces per year—has tripled its sales of timepieces, notably with a striking selection of ladies' complication watches.

In fact, for the very lovely ladies' pieces issued, this house has earned its bragging rights. Grace and refinement are hallmarks of this brand's watches. Time becomes secondary when you slip on a Van Cleef & Arpels watch, which is more like a jewel than a timepiece. The company, which was acquired by the Richemont group in 1999, is also known for its secret watches with quartz mechanisms hidden under jewel studding. The Cadenas is another emblematic Van Cleef & Arpels timepiece. The lock theme was initially explored by the brand in 1935 and has since inspired an astonishing snake-chain bracelet that closes with a timepiece lock and a snap hook. The Cadenas has been released in a whole slew of different versions (in leather, with a checked bracelet, etc.) and is available from $3,550 for the steel model, up to $14,200 for yellow gold. The same principle applies to the Alhambra Vintage watch, which was inspired by a famous line of clover-shaped jewelry originally launched in 1974. Introduced in 2005, the Alhambra Vintage features a clover-shaped gold case and an onyx dial on a black satin strap ($6,250).

In a more horological realm, in 2006 the company launched the richly decorated Complications Poétiques line, with themes inspired by its *haute joaillerie* collections. With a Jaeger-LeCoultre mechanical movement fitted with a disk that makes a full rotation every 24 hours, the 4 seasons, fairies, and ballerinas, etc. parade by over a 365-day cycle. One of the most well-executed pieces is undoubtedly the Midnight in Paris, where an aventurine starry sky turns on its frost-covered blue quartz dial ($64,000 for rose-gold case on an alligator strap). In the same spirit, the jeweler offers tourbillon watches distinguished by their dials, sumptuously ornamented with mother-of-pearl marquetry, raised enamel, and precious stones, which are successful among collectors in Asia.

Cadenas.
Quartz watch.

The Art of the Dial

For the past four years, Van Cleef & Arpels has applied a jeweler's savoir faire to a few exceptional timepieces with watch faces decorated like paintings. Hummingbirds, Californian landscapes, butterflies, peacocks... on these dials just a few centimeters wide, tiny, poetic worlds come into being.

Tourbillon Colibri.
Mechanical watch with tourbillon.

LOUIS VUITTON

Tambour Large GMT.
Automatic watch displaying a
second time zone.

Tambour in Black LV277.
Automatic chronograph.

Emprise LV.
Quartz watch.

AN UNEXPECTED SUCCESS

In 2002 Louis Vuitton launched its first watch, the Tambour. Thanks to a comprehensive collection and an especially high-quality product, the global leader in luxury goods managed to confound skeptical timepiece specialists and pull off its gamble.

Louis Vuitton's first watch was launched in Tokyo for the 2002 opening of the company's largest-ever store. With 132 watches sold in the store's first hour of business, the Tambour was off to a rip-roaring start. Within six weeks, the company had sold its entire supply of watches intended for a six-month period, and found itself facing a seven-thousand-person, six-month waiting list for an out-of-stock product. A stunned Yves Carcelle, president of Louis Vuitton, could only state that the company had "thought the Tambour's launch would be a success, but not to this point," while the naysayers who saw the Tambour as nothing more than another designer watch in an oversaturated market were left with egg on their faces. A year after its initial release, the Tambour was still going strong. In fact, by 2003 production was tripled, to thirty thousand pieces, and the company estimated sixty thousand watches would be needed to meet public demand for the Tambour. Though Louis Vuitton has stopped releasing its production figures, current production of the Tambour is estimated at fifty thousand pieces a year.

One of the reasons for the Tambour's success is that Louis Vuitton never enters a new market—be it in shoes or ready-to-wear—without absorbing the necessary technical know-how. For starters, the celebrated luggage manufacturer created its own timepiece production division in La Chaux-de-Fonds, Switzerland. As a leading entity of the LVMH group, Louis Vuitton was also able to form synergies and draw on the experience of other LVMH watch companies such as TAG Heuer and Zenith. Most important, the company chose to put its money into a timeless product that would reflect an authentic mastery of horological principles, rather than on a mere fashion watch fated to go out of style. It's no surprise, then, that creating the Tambour took two years of hard work on the part of six design teams and an investment of more than $1 million in research and development.

The outcome of all this work is a convincing model that provides a faithful representation of the Louis Vuitton spirit. Formally, for instance, the Tambour is relatively simple. Its steel case is formed by two thick disks that give the watch a particularly tactile dimension. Equally true to the Vuitton style, the chromatic palette used for the Tambour's dials and bracelets displays exquisite finesse (brown, taupe, sand, etc.), and features the emblematic colors of Vuitton luggage and its monogram canvas. And true to Vuitton's reputation for sophistication, the calibers equipping its roughly thirty

Tambour Heures Mystérieuses.
Watch with ghost hands and
automatic movement.

Tourbillon Tambour Monogram.
Skeleton mechanical movement
with tourbillon at 6 o'clock.
Rose gold case.

Tambour LV Cup Régate.
Automatic chronograph with fly-
back function and countdown
timer.

timepieces are not limited to quartz. One can buy a Vuitton automatic chronograph, for instance, starting at about $5,300. The Tambour in Black automatic chronograph uses Zenith's famous El Primero caliber as a base for its movement and is certified as a chronometer by the COSC. Here we see Vuitton's attention to detail in full force: the movement's rotor is finely worked and decorated with the initials LV ($16,200). Other notable pieces include the Tambour GMT, with dual time zones ($3,250 on a navy blue alligator strap); the Tambour Diving, which is water resistant to one thousand feet and features an ETA 28 95 automatic movement (from $4,580); and the Tambour LV Cup Regatta, an automatic chronograph with a fly-back function and a countdown timer ($8,600 with a brown dial).

Stepping beyond the above models, in 2004 Louis Vuitton launched a particularly risky attempt at the most difficult timepiece complication by issuing a new Tambour featuring a skeleton tourbillon. Once again the gamble paid off, thanks to Vuitton's decision to offer customers boundless opportunity to personalize these superbly executed watches. Buyers may choose not only the metal used for the watch's case or the color of the shagreen bracelet, they can also select the shape of the movement's third wheel bridge. Options include having the bridge shaped like its owner's initials or set with diamonds or precious stones. This concept may seem ridiculous at first glance, but it is actually the epitome of chic. But you'll have to plan on spending $190,000 and waiting six months to get your hands on one of these beauties. In the same vein, in 2009 the leather goods company launched a mysterious hours watch that should also be completely customizable.

Unfortunately the new Speedy line of square-cased watches is less convincing. The neo-retro dials on Speedy models are said to be inspired by the automotive field, and bear distinct resemblances to the Monaco watch by TAG Heuer, which is also owned by the LVMH group. More impressive is the Emprise, the first watch created by Marc Jacobs, the artistic director of the ready-to-wear fashion line of the Vuitton brand. This very 1970s-style collection offers both rectangular and square cases that are especially chic in yellow gold with pure, understated black dials (from $11,400 with a quartz movement).

HARRY WINSTON

THOROUGHBRED WATCHES

For twenty years, the New York jeweler has successfully wooed high-end timepiece lovers with an immediately identifiable style, complicated movements devised in collaboration with independent watchmakers, and frequently remarkable limited editions.

Why bother making watches when you sell diamond-studded jewelry for several million dollars apiece? For the simple reason that Ronald Winston, son of celebrated New York jeweler Harry Winston, likes watches. In 1989 the company launched Ultimate Timepieces, its first watch collection, including a particularly luxurious bi-retrograde perpetual calendar developed with two independent watchmakers, Jean-Marc Wiederrecht and Roger Dubuis. By being the first to combine a perpetual calendar with a retrograde hand, Harry Winston clearly demonstrated its commitment to producing technically accomplished models conceived in collaboration with the best contemporary watchmakers. In fact, the retrograde hand soon became a house specialty, along with the company's use of a whole range of materials rarely seen in watchmaking. Materials now largely associated with Harry Winston watches include rhodium (used for the 1991 Galatea), platinum (used for the 1998 Ocean, a diving chronograph water resistant to 330 feet), and Zalium (a hypoallergenic alloy developed in the aerospace industry and used in 2004 and 2005 to make the cases of the Project Z1 and Project Z2).

In 2001, Harry Winston's renown as a timepiece company was stepped up a notch by the launch of the Opus series, an annual limited edition of a single, truly innovative model conceived in collaboration with an independent watchmaker. The Opus series was doubly unusual. First, a brand rarely chooses to call attention to the fact that it has collaborated with a third party to develop its movements. Second, Harry Winston turned that collaborative spirit into a full-fledged marketing concept by putting two signatures on the Opus.

Owned by the Canadian company Aber Diamonds Corporation since 2004, Harry Winston currently produces about five thousand watches a year. The permanent collection simultaneously offers jewelry watches and more complicated pieces, such as the Excenter line. Launched in 2002, these watches are characterized by their off-center dials. The Excenter Biretro, for instance, is truly representative of Winston watches ($52,900). This diamond-set ladies' watch features an automatic movement and retrograde indications of the seconds and the days of the week. The Excenter Timezone is an innovative model, providing dual time zones on a retrograde twenty-four-hour counter, as well as a day/night indication based on the first time zone ($26,300 in yellow gold). The Excenter Tourbillon, which retails for $122,800 in white gold, is equally impressive. Launched in 2005, this hand-wound caliber with a frequency of 28,800

Excenter Tourbillon.
Hand-wound mechanical movement, tourbillon, double retrograde power reserve indicator. Platinum case.

Ocean Dual Time.
Automatic watch with dual time zone.

Excenter Biretro.
Automatic ladies' watch with retrograde seconds and date indicator. White gold case set with diamonds.

Premier Excenter Perpetual Calendar.
Automatic watch with perpetual calendar and moon phases with retrograde display.

vibrations per hour was developed with English watchmaker Peter Speake-Marin. One of the Excenter Tourbillon's particularities is the retrograde double power-reserve indicator on its back, which keeps track of the watch's nearly five days of autonomy. Moreover, because the tourbillon cage's rotational system is inside rather than outside the movement, the Excenter's tourbillon is one of the most accurate and stable tourbillons on the market. The vintage model of this family, the Excenter Perpetual Calendar, underwent a slight makeover in 2007 ($53,600).

These complications can be found in the Ocean line in a more solid, sporty design (retrograde hands, tourbillon, chronograph, etc.), as in the Ocean Dual Time, an automatic model with second time zone that won an award at the Grand Prix d'Horlogerie de Genève in 2008 (around $41,000 in rose gold).

Finally, Winston also offers some *haute horlogerie* pieces in small limited editions: a flying tourbillon with minute repeater and Westminster carillon; an automatic glissière tourbillon, etc.

Poetic Opuses

The Opus I, conceived in 2001 with François-Paul Journe, was an eighteen-piece limited edition featuring six automatic pieces with five-day power reserves, six resonance chronometers, and six tourbillons with constant-force winding mechanisms. Though the Opus I disconcerted the timepiece business, the jeweler didn't abandon its plans, instead launching successive models which have sold out in the $75,000 to $175,000 price range. In 2002 the brand collaborated with Antoine Preziuso to create the Opus II, a series of twenty-four tourbillons, twelve of which feature a perpetual calendar on the back of their cases, with a lid beneath which the day of the week and the date are displayed. But it was the 2003 Opus III, conceived with Vianney Halter, that left the watch world speechless. This out-landish model could be taken for anything other than a watch. Rather than hands, the Opus III features six portholes through which the hours, minutes, seconds, and jump date appear. It is the first mechanical watch to provide an entirely numerical display. Despite a hefty price of $77,900 for each pink-gold model, the fifty-five pieces in the Opus III series flew off the shelves. The eighteen Opus IV watches designed in 2004 with Christophe Claret met with equal success. The Opus IV boasted a double-sided case displaying a tourbillon and a minute repeater with a cathedral gong on its face, a large moon phase, and a calendar on the reverse. As for the 2005 Opus V, created with Félix Baumgartner, its three-dimensional time display reinvented how we read time. The Opus V is a "satellite hour" watch featuring a retrograde minute hand. The time is displayed via three little blocks placed as satellites on a rotational system. The blocks reveal the time by successively moving in front of the appropriate minutes. In other words, the wheel of time "turns" before the Opus V owner's eyes. This hundred-piece limited edition made an impression. Turning to a futuristic style, Frédéric Garinaud's 2008 Opus VIII features a digital display sustained by an all-mechanical caliber. As for the Opus IX, created by Jean-Marc Wiederrecht and Éric Giroud, it is content with providing the hour and the minutes, yet in a rather unconventional manner. It is a capsule watch, housed in a glass cylinder, with neither case nor dial nor hands, where the time is displayed in a linear fashion alongside two tracks of diamonds. It is available in a limited edition of one hundred.

ABOVE: The Opus V.
OPPOSITE: The Opus IX.

ZENITH

Since its acquisition by LVMH in 1999, this watch manufacturer, founded in Le Locle in 1865, has radically revamped its collections. Zenith now offers a line of highly desirable timepieces supported by exceptional movements, including the world-famous El Primero.

In ten years, LVMH, the world leader in luxury goods, has spared no effort (nor investment) to revive this august Swiss manufacturer, whose image had been in decline for several years. Indeed, when LVMH took over, Zenith's image was in a nosedive; the company had changed hands four times between 1969 and 1984, its collections were overdone, and its watch designs were simply devoid of interest. Zenith did have one thing going for it, however: the company has always produced the majority of its movements' components in-house. And these movements included one of the most famous watch calibers in the world, the El Primero. Introduced in 1969, the El Primero is accurate to 1/10th of a second and was the first self-wound chronograph to oscillate 36,000 times per hour. The Zenith catalog also boasted the caliber Élite, an ultrathin movement developed by the company in 1994 that oscillates 28,800 times per hour.

In 2001 Thierry Nataf was appointed president and CEO of Zenith. Nataf resolutely moved the brand upmarket into the world of luxury products while capitalizing on its accumulated technical know-how. Up until Nataf's departure in 2009, the company looked afresh at its collections, hoping to inject glamour and modernity, both of which were sorely lacking. For starters, the company stopped selling its celebrated caliber El Primero to other watch brands (Rolex, Panerai, etc.) in order to reclaim it as an exclusive Zenith product. El Primero became the cornerstone of the company's new strategy, a base for developing new mechanisms, but also the heart of the company's image. Zenith even started opening its watch dials to show the El Primero in action. The aptly named Open concept signaled Zenith's rebirth in the world of mechanical watchmaking.

Zenith's revamped collections were structured according to the basic principles of the luxury-goods market: to offer customers a fantasy by selling desirable products indicative of a comfortable lifestyle at a variety of price points. In this respect Zenith has certainly pulled off its gamble—but at the risk of breaking from its traditional clientele, which did not identify with the more extravagant, sometimes-flashy collections developed by the Locle workshop. The appointment of Jean-Frédéric Dufour to the head of the brand in May of 2009 should put its lines back on a more classic track.

Although the company does not disclose any business figures, it appears to produce around eighteen thousand watches a year. Zenith's roughly twenty in-house calibers encompass the principal watchmaking styles, from the plain automatic watch with three hands (about $6,000) to elaborate complications, such as the minute repeater and the tourbillon (between $300,000 and $740,000). Since 2006 Zenith has maintained a presence in sport watches with the Defy line; within three years this line accounted for one-third of the

Class Moonphase.
Automatic watch with date, small seconds, and moon phase display.

Chronomaster Open.
Automatic chronograph with power reserve indicator.

Defy Xtreme.

Academy Open.
Watch with minute repeater.

Elite Class Reserve de Marche.
Ultraflat automatic watch with
power reserve indicator.

*Primero Class Open Traveller
Multicity Alarm.*
Automatic chronograph with 24
time zones and alarm function.

Vintage 1969 Originals.
Automatic chronograph in steel.

company's sales. Its program includes oversize cases, high-tech materials (titanium, carbon fiber, etc.) and in-house movements with functions ranging from the simplest to the most complicated. At the low end of the price scale is the Defy Classic, with small seconds and date that runs on the Elite caliber (about $6,800). In 2008 the brand launched an *haute horlogerie* model, the Defy Xtreme Zero-G, with a transgenic design that features a gyroscopic cage tourbillon that seems weightless. What's more, this "zero-gravity" watch, based on the El Primero automatic caliber, is water resistant to approximately 3,281 feet ($350,000).

In a more urban mode, the Academy line brings together highly sophisticated complication models. The mind-boggling Academy tourbillon chronograph, launched in 2004, is the only one on the market that reaches thirty-six thousand alternations per hour ($186,000 in platinum on leather strap). There are also minute repeaters and perpetual calendars with highly polished finishing.

Among the simpler pieces, the Chronomaster XXT Open (starting around $8,300) with power reserve display is one of the brand's best sellers. Aside from the excellence of its automatic caliber, visible at ten o'clock, the Open El Primero chronograph, which has been the object of twenty-one patents, embodies a very contemporary elegance (around $8,000). It is available in several models (moon phase, tourbillon, large date display). Also well regarded is the Class line, which emphasizes simplicity with several variations based on the Elite and El Primero movements. The automatic model with power reserve display and dual time zone is available for about $6,000. The Class Moonphase released in 2009 is also understated, with large date display, small seconds, and moon phase that run on the new extrathin Elite 691 movement (about $9,000).

Finally, to celebrate the fortieth anniversary of the El Primero, Zenith launched several limited editions, spawning the success of New Vintage, which revisits the original model without being affectedly trendy. These are fine pieces.

"Women, I love you."

Zenith is one of the rare watchmakers to have built a real collection of ladies' timepieces. No quartz here, nor scaled-down men's styles, but 100 percent feminine pieces built exclusively on the house's mechanical calibers. In fact, three years after the women's collection debuted in the early 2000s, it accounted for 30 percent of the brand's sales. With a price range of just under $6,000 to nearly $450,000, this line includes beautiful complications like this fashionable tourbillon, dressed in pearls and diamonds.

FOLLOWING PAGES: *Academy El Primero Concept Tourbillon.*
Automatic chronograph with tourbillon.

It's in the Air: Genetically Modified Watches

Swollen timepieces, over-sized dials and an excess of functions . . . The watchmaking world's "new guard" is producing models that could be anything—except a watch.

In the twenty-first century, are watchmakers fighting the battle between the Ancients and the Moderns yet again? It would seem so.

Over the last two or three years a new generation of self-confident, assertive designers has emerged. Atypical and ambitious, their goal is nothing more or less than to distinguish themselves by offering "another vision" of contemporary watch making.

Beyond the designers' powerful personalities, this stance—half-heroic and half-unconscious (and all the more so since the 2008 global economic crisis) —has given them media attention inversely proportional to their economic clout, which is virtually nonexistent. Indeed, production rarely exceeds a few hundred pieces. These minimalist collections are distributed on a limited basis, if at all, and the prices are often stratospheric.

Nonetheless, this new wave of watch making is emblematic of a time that loves nothing more than destroying today what it loved yesterday. And the reverse. The details . . .

OPPOSITE: The HM2 by MBF in white gold.

MBF

Maximilian Büsser & Friends (MBF) makes timekeeping machines, not watches. Since 2006, when Max Büsser, former Opus designer at Harry Winston, founded his own company, he and his friends have been designing an unconventional "Horological Machine" every year.

No. 1 resembles a two-headed hydra, with the minute and power reserve indicator (right) separated from the raised tourbillon (center) and from the hours (left).

No. 2 is a two-eyed UFO. One dial features concentric jump hours and retrograde minutes and the other, a concentric moon phase and retrograde date.

No. 3 has reversed the movement (the rotor is above). Intelligent minds will be able to reach the hours on one side and minutes on the other, thanks to two prominent cones.

New toys for big boys.

ABOVE: the HM2.
OPPOSITE: the HM3.

ROMAIN JÉRÔME

This small brand appeared in 2007 with the launch of the Titanic watch, the first of its kind to incorporate a fragment of the renowned liner's rusted hull in its case.

Since then, the watch has resurfaced in a host of versions, including a spectacular skeleton model with chronograph and tourbillon, launched in 2009.

Jerome's Day & Night is equally radical. It has two tourbillons and—the ultimate mark of luxury—it does not tell time.

The Moon Dust DNA is less morbid, with a cratered dial made of real moon dust. It is for those who live for stories, who love watches that tell a tale.

ABOVE: The Day & Night.
OPPOSITE: The Moon Dust DNA Simple.

URWERK

Founded in 1997 by watchmaker Félix Baumgartner and designer Martin Frei, Urwerk is *the* up-and-coming Swiss watch brand.

Why? First, because the models, which resemble flying saucers, have a strong identity. And second, because the satellite time display is both innovative and (relatively) legible.

The best-known model is the UR 103. The skeleton version presents four satellites marching past an arc of minutes.

The UR 201 has also been well received. It incorporates a telescoping minute hand that travels across the hour markers.

Urwerk launched the CC1 in September 2009, its first watch featuring linear the time and minute indicators. The digital readout seconds display is visible through an aperture. It's a futurist must-have.

ABOVE: The UR202.
OPPOSITE: The CC1.

Academic Subjects

Founded in Switzerland in 1984, the Horological Academy of Independent Creators (Académie horlogère des créateurs indépendants, or AHCI), is composed of twenty-eight watchmakers from ten different countries. They are unusual—often idealistic and not terribly organized—but each produces artisan watches in his own little corner of the world. Most of their creations include exquisite complications.

The AHCI is an incubator where watch lovers can discover a triple-axis tourbillon (Thomas Prescher), poetic jump-hour designs (Vincent Calabrese), a huge moon phase in lapis lazuli (Antoine Preziuso), erotic watches (Svend Andersen), and, simply, masterpieces of mechanical perfection, such as the models produced in extremely limited editions by the great Philippe Dufour.

Every year, AHCI members show their work in a booth on the second floor of the Basel Watch Fair. It's definitely worth a stop. Otherwise, for a taste of their designs, visit the academy's Web site, www.ahci.ch.

OPPOSITE: the Simplicity by Philippe Dufour.

Price Guide

Some people need a rare watch graced with the patina of time to start or complete their collection. Others may succumb to the vintage trend in order to strap on a model they'll be sure never to see on anyone else's wrist.

Whatever the reason, the antique watch market is drawing an increasing number of enthusiasts. After all, antique watches carry the spirit of an era, a style, and the craft of the watchmakers who constructed them.

This price chart by expert Romain Réa, horology specialist for more than fifteen years, lists the estimated values of twenty-nine models based on current trends on the collector's market.

The Longines Lindbergh aviator watch in steel with white enamel-and-silverface, hour angle, blued-steel Breguet needle, and large second hand, mechanical movement 18.69N.
Circa 1930. $23,000/$38,000.

All prices cited in this chapter are given as an approximate reference.

BELL & ROSS
Space 1 by SINN - 800 €/1 200 €
Chronographe tonneau en acier avec lunette tournante intérieure
(couronne à 10 heures), cadran noir avec indication 24 heures
à midi, double guichet date, mouvement automatique.
Circa 1990.

BLANCPAIN
Harwood – 1 500 €/2 500 €
Première montre-bracelet automatique, boîtier tonneau en or sans
couronne de remontage, cadran argent avec chiffres Breguet or,
indication de marche à 6 heures, mouvement à marteau,
équipé de deux ressorts à buter. *Circa 1925.*

BOUCHERON
Polyplan – 3 000 €/4 000 €
Montre en or gris, polyplan cintré curvex,
cadran deux tons avec chiffres arabes appliqués,
mouvement mécanique.
Circa 1940.

BREGUET
Chrono pilote – 7 000 €/9 000 €
Chronographe bracelet en acier, boîtier rond avec lunette tournante
graduée de 1 à 12, cadran noir trois compteurs avec totalisateurs
15 minutes et 12 heures signés Breguet, mouvement mécanique
calibre Valjoux, capsule antimagnétique, fond vissé.
Circa 1960.

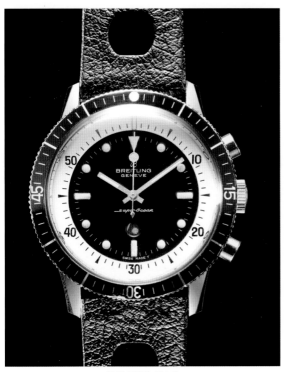

BREITLING
Super Ocean – $1,800/$3,000
Steel diving chronograph, graduated rotating bezel, chronograph push
buttons to calculate decompression times in minutes, black dial with
sweep second hand and aperture indicating chronograph activation,
Valjoux Caliber 7731 mechanical movement.
Circa 1970.

BULGARI
Plastic – $1,100/$1,500
Rare black plastic watch, black dial with gold numerals and
gold baton hands, gold rotor movement, skeleton back.
Series limited to three thousand three hundred pieces.
Circa 1993.

CARTIER
Baignoire Jumbo – $10,700/$16,700
Cambered oval watch in gold, cream dial with hand-painted
numerals, blued steel hands, mechanical movement.
Circa 1950.

CHANEL
Première – $700/$1,050.
Ladies' watch with a gold and octagonal rectangular case,
inspired by the outline of Place Vendôme,
with black dial, quartz movement, metal bracelet woven
with strips of leather.
Circa 1987.

BELL & ROSS

Space 1 by SINN – $950/$1,400

Steel tonneau chronograph with interior rotating bezel
(crown at ten o'clock), black dial with twenty-four-hour display,
double aperture date, automatic movement.

Circa 1990.

BLANCPAIN

Harwood – $1,800/$3,100

First automatic wristwatch. Gold tonneau case without a winding
crown. Silver dial with gold Breguet numerals, working reserve
indication at six o'clock. Movement with hammer-winding system
and two backstop springs.

Circa 1925.

BOUCHERON

Polyplan – $3,500/$4,700

Gray gold wristwatch, curvex polyplan,
two-shades dial with applied Arabic numerals,
mechanical movement.

Circa 1940.

BREGUET

Chrono Pilote · $8,200/$10,500

Chronograph with steel bracelet, round case with rotating bezel
graduated from one to twelve, black dial with three subdials and
fifteen-minute and twelve-hour totalizers by Breguet, Valjoux caliber
mechanical movement, antimagnetic cap, screwed-down back.

Circa 1960.

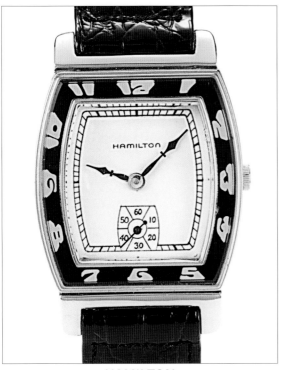

HAMILTON
Coronado – $2,200/$2,800
Gold tonneau wristwatch, black enamel bezel, flexible
straight lugs. Cream dial with railroad scale and small sec-
ond hand, caliber 979 mechanical movement.
Circa 1929.

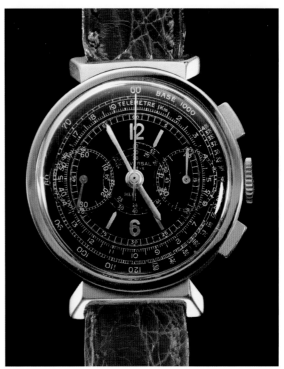

HERMÈS
Compax – $4,900/$7,350
Chronograph wristwatch in rose gold.
Black dial with two counters and a tachometric scale.
Universal Genève mechanical movement.
Circa 1930.

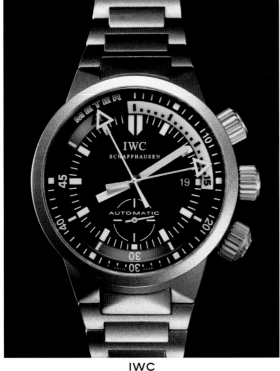

IWC
GST Deep One – $12,250/$18,400
Diving watch with mechanical depth gauge (145 feet).
Black dial with small sweep second hand and date display,
depth gauge area in yellow. Automatic movement with a
split time counter.
Circa 2000.

JAEGER-LECOULTRE
Power Reserve – $2,900/$4,900
Gold round watch, with crown at the back of the case,
silver dial, automatic movement with 497 caliber.
Circa 1955.

FRANÇOIS-PAUL JOURNE
Tourbillon Sourverain "Souscription" – $55,000/$89,000
Platinum case with one-minute tourbillon and constant force
device, power reserve at twelve o'clock, constant force device
at six o'clock and tourbillon cage at nine o'clock, mechanical
movement, skeleton back.
Circa 1998.

LONGINES
Conquest "20th Olympic Games, Munich"
– $1,600/$2,800
Single push-button steel chronograph, screwed-down back.
Silver dial with counter at three o'clock. Caliber 326
mechanical movement.
1972.

ULYSSE NARDIN
Water-resistant chronograph – $9,800/$14,600
Rose gold chronograph wristwatch with horn lugs and round
push buttons. White dial with two counters.
Caliber Valjoux 23 mechanical movement.
Circa 1950.

OMEGA
Constellation – $2,100 / $2,700
Rose gold round watch with curved lugs, cream "spider"
dial, arrowhead hour markers and gold hands, caliber 28.10
automatic movement, chronometer-certified.
Circa 1955.

PATEK PHILIPPE
Curvex "Guillermin" – $9,800/$14,000
Rose gold rectangular wristwatch with furled lugs and screw-down clasps. Cream dial with rose gold baton markers and hands. Caliber 9 shaped mechanical movement.
Circa 1945.

PORSCHE DESIGN
Kon Tiki Reedition – $700/$1,000
Steel wristwatch, round curved case, blue dial with date stamp, large sweep second hand and automatic movement.
Circa 2000.

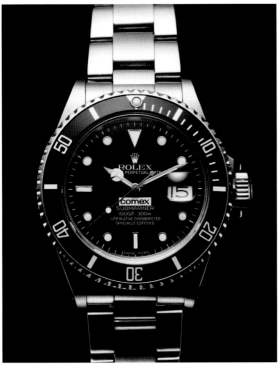

ROLEX
Submariner Comex – $12,000/$18,000
Steel diving watch, rotating bezel, back of case engraved with Comex numbers, black dial with date display, automatic movement.
Circa 1980.

TAG HEUER
Bundeswehr Chronograph – $2,100/$3,300
Steel chronograph with rotating bezel, black dial with two subdials, red 3/H (hydrogen isotope as per NATO specifications), mechanical movement with Valjoux caliber.
Circa 1970.

TISSOT
PR 516 – $700/$1,100
Steel chronograph, tonneau case, red and white pulsimeter.
Black dial with two rally counters. Caliber LWC 872
mechanical movement.
Circa 1970.

VACHERON CONSTANTIN
Chronograph – $23,000/$35,000
Round pink gold chronograph with tear-shaped lugs,
cream-colored dial with two subdials, tachometric scale,
434 caliber mechanical movement with column wheels.
Circa 1940.

ZENITH
Port Royal – $4,900/$7,350
Rose gold round wristwatch. Dial in two shades of gold,
with gold hands. Caliber 135 chronometer mechanical
movement.
Circa 1965.

The Blancpain Fifty Fathoms diving watch
used by Jacques Cousteau in *The Silent World*.
Rotating bezel, graduated turning glass,
and black face with luminescent numbers and index,
automatic movement AS with antimagnetic capsule.
Circa 1950. $5,000/$8,000.

Upkeep: Standing the Test of Time

Whether mechanical, automatic, or quartz, watches
are just like cars: they need to be serviced.
Let's examine some common issues that arise
with watches and what you'll
need to do—and avoid doing—to ensure
a long life for your timepiece.

Harold Lloyd in *Safety Last!* (1923),
directed by Fred Newmeyer and Sam Taylor.

Mechanical and automatic watches are far more fragile than quartz watches.

True. Nothing beats the robustness, accuracy, and reliable water resistance of a quartz watch. Mechanical and automatic watches are far from being indestructible. In fact, their solidity is in inverse proportion to the number of functions they have. Clearly stated, the more complicated functions a watch has (tourbillon, perpetual calendar, minute repeater, chronograph, etc.), the more you'll have to baby it. In general, hand-wound and automatic mechanical calibers are vulnerable to violent shocks, heat, and sudden temperature change. It is worth noting, however, that a hand-wound mechanical watch is generally more accurate and less fragile than one with an automatic movement, because its movement does not contain a rotor and does not have the same level of spring tension. A quartz watch should not encounter any water or shock-resistance problems.

A quartz watch's battery must be changed at least every three years.

True. Beyond that time period, the battery is likely to run, spreading battery acid and corroding the circuit, and effectively rendering the watch worthless. In order to avoid damaging the waterproof joints when opening the case, it is best to have the battery changed by a watch specialist. The cost of having a battery changed varies wildly, with little justification. Eight to eighteen dollars will get you a battery change and nothing else. The prohibitive fees charged by watch brands (between $60 and $120) include a range of supplementary operations. In that price range, a battery replacement should include a movement checkup, replacement of all the waterproof joints, testing of the watch's water resistance, and a cleaning of the case and the bracelet.

A mechanical or automatic watch must be serviced every four or five years.

True. This is indispensable to avoid the works prematurely wearing out, and to ensure that the watch's water resistance and working condition are still optimal. A watch repairer thoroughly services a watch by "undressing" it, then "dressing" it again, i.e. by taking apart the movement, cleaning all the components with ultrasounds, checking all the parts and replacing the defective ones, oiling the works, testing the watch's working order, changing the waterproof joints, and cleaning and polishing the case and the bracelet. By the time you reclaim your watch, it will be as good as new. Depending on the brand, servicing will cost you between $375 and $750. In general, watch servicing is guaranteed for one year.

You can have your watch serviced or repaired by any watchmaker.
False. An unqualified watchmaker who is not authorized by leading watch brands will not own the tools and parts necessary for the standard upkeep, servicing, and repair of the watch. Moreover, any problem you run into will be particularly costly, as watch brands do not guarantee repairs by unauthorized dealers. The simplest solution is to take your watch to the brand's official dealer, who will most frequently send it back to the manufacturer. This has the distinct advantage of avoiding any risk to the dealer or to you, but the sizable disadvantage of an excessively long two- to three-month waiting period. Another solution is to have the watch repaired on site, so long as the dealer employs an authorized watchmaker. This is quicker and tailor-made to your needs. Some dealers even lend customers a courtesy watch while their watches are being serviced.

Mechanical sport watches aren't made to be worn while you play sports.
True and false. It all depends on the type of sport being engaged in. Any sport involving repeated up-and-down motion (dirt biking, golf, tennis, squash) can eventually seriously shake up a mechanical or automatic watch. In these cases, if you're an intensive sportsman, it's best to leave your prized timepiece in the locker room and strap on a quartz watch.

A water-resistant watch can be worn twenty-four hours a day, even in the shower and the tub.
False. Water pressure from the showerhead can damage the most robust mechanism. And we won't even get into soap or shower gel infiltrations, or the thermal shock that can ruin a watch if it's plunged into piping hot bathwater. Always take your watch off before you step into the bathroom. And don't wear it to the beach, where thermal shock will seriously damage its mechanism if you dive into cold water after having let your watch roast in the sun for a while. For the same reason, watches do not do well with saunas and steam rooms and the ice-cold showers they are traditionally followed by.

Rubber bracelets are more resistant than leather bracelets.
False. When a rubber bracelet is extensively worn in the sun, it is extremely likely to stain, to lose its color, or even to begin cracking, particularly if it is made in Asia. Rubber is also sensitive to chlorine, gas, and household solvents. As for leather bracelets, note that they must not be worn on a daily basis: they must be allowed to "breathe" between uses in order for the humidity collected from the wearer's wrist to be evacuated. Also note that so-called waterproof leather is never truly waterproof. So don't ever bathe with a crocodile. A crocodile bracelet, that is . . .

The Watch Lover's Address Book

Want to track down a unique timepiece?
Have an antique clock repaired?
Buy a secondhand watch?
Choose a made-to-measure strap?
You'll find a list of the best places
in the business on the following pages.

Watchmaker's Dress, engraving by Nicolas de Larmessin's workshop,
late seventeenth/early eighteenth century. Biblothèque Nationale, Paris.

High-end retailers

France

CHRONOPASSION

French complication watch specialist (Audemars Piguet, Breguet, and Richard Mille). Laurent Picciotto also carries unique Girard-Perregaux pieces.
271, rue Saint-Honoré, 75001 Paris
Tel.: + 33 (1) 42 60 50 72
Fax: + 33 (1) 49 27 31 48
Web site: www.chronopassion.fr
E-mail: chronoweb@chronopassion.fr

ARIJE

50, rue Pierre-Charron, 75008 Paris
Tel.: + 33 (1) 47 20 72 40
Fax: + 33 (1) 47 20 42 01
Web site: www.arije.com
E-mail: shop@arije.com

DUBAIL

21, Place Vendôme, 75001 Paris
Tel.: + 33 (1) 42 61 11 17
Fax: + 33 (1) 42 61 07 44
Web site: www.dubail.fr

LES MONTRES PASSY

40, rue de Passy, 75016 Paris
Tel.: + 33 (1) 53 92 51 61
Web site: www.lesmontrespassy.com
E-mail: montrepassy@wanadoo.fr

ROYAL QUARTZ

10, rue Royale, 75008 Paris
Tel.: + 33 (1) 42 60 58 58
Fax: + 33 (1) 47 03 00 39
Web site: www.royal-quartz.com

KRONOMETRY 1999

4, boulevard de la Croisette, 06400 Cannes
Tel.: + 33 (4) 97 06 69 70
Fax: 0147 03 00 39
Web site: www.kronometry1999.com
E-mail: info@kronometry1999.com

Switzerland

LES AMBASSADEURS

This temple of Swiss watchmaking carries watches by fifteen leading companies (Blancpain, Cartier, A. Lange & Söhne, Ulysse Nardin, Vacheron Constantin, etc.).
39, rue du Rhône, 1204 Geneva
Tel.: + 41 (22) 318 62 22
Web site: www.lesambassadeurs.ch
E-mail: geneve@lesambassadeurs.ch

MEZGER AG

Uhren und Juwelen, 4051 Basel
Tel.: + 41 (61) 206 99 55
Fax: + 41 (61) 206 99 56
Web site: www.mezger.ch
E-mail: urs.mezger@mezger.ch

United States

WESTIME

John Simonian loves complicated watches. He carries Audemars Piguet, Richard Mille, and Urwerk pieces.
254 North Rodeo Drive, Beverly Hills, CA 90210
Tel.: 310 271 0000
Fax: 310 271 3091
Web site: www.westime.net
E-mail: sales@westimewatches.com

HESS FINE ART

1131, 4th Street N., St. Petersburg, FL 33701
Tel.: 800 922 4377
Web site: www.hessfineart.com
E-mail: hessfine@hessfineart.com

Japan

• TAKARADO CO, LTD.

Founded in 1930, this store carries many jewelry watches (Cartier, Chopard, Franck Müller, etc.).
2-4-4, Gofuku-cho J-420-0031, Shizuoka City
Tel.: + 81 (54) 254 0141
Fax: +81 (54) 251 2660
Web site: www.takarado.co.jp
E-mail: info@takarado.co.jp

Taiwan

• TIEN WEN WATCH CO.

Unique Haute Horlogerie pieces and exceptional limited editions by Audemars Piguet, Cartier, Piaget, and others.
113, Chung Cheng Road, Taichung
Tel.: 00 (88) 64 222 56476
Fax: 00 (88) 64 222 38038

Made-to-measure

France

• L'ATELIER DU BRACELET PARISIEN

The "Paris watchstrap workshop" specializes in custom-made watchstraps displaying top craftsmanship, classic or exotic leathers (anaconda, ostrich, llama, etc.), and a wide range of colors.
28, place du Marché Saint-Honoré, 75001 Paris
Tel.: + 33 (1) 42 86 13 70
Fax: + 33 (1) 40 20 43 46
Web site: www.abp-paris.com
E-mail: info.abp@wanadoo.fr

• CAMILLE FOURNET

3, rue d'Alger, 75001 Paris
Tel.: 01 40 20 14 04
Web site: www.camillefournet.com

Switzerland

• GOLAY SPIERER

This specialist in custom-made watches lets you choose whether you want a simple or a complicated movement (tourbillon, minute repeater, etc.). Plan on waiting a year before your watch is finished.
2, rue Saint-Victor, 1227 Carouge - Geneva
Tel.: + 41 (22) 301 78 58
Fax: + 41 (22) 301 78 60
Web site: www.golay-spierer.ch
E-mail: info@golay-spierer.ch

United States

• SUI GENERIS LLC

53 East 58th Street, New York, NY 10022
Tel.: 212 935 3786
Fax: 212 935 3796
Web site: www.suigeneris.com

Antique timepiece sales and repairs

France

● LA PENDULERIE

This is the place to go if you're looking for eighteenth- and nineteenth-century clocks by Breguet, Antide Janvier, Le Paute, or Lepine. You'll also find a workshop for restoring clocks on the premises.
134, rue du Faubourg-Saint-Honoré,
75008 Paris
Tel.: + 33 (1) 45 61 44 55
Fax: + 33 (1) 45 61 44 54
Web site: www.lapendulerie.fr

● PHILIPPE PRUTNER

One of the best restorers of timepieces (clocks, watches) and antique scientific instruments (astronomical and topographical) in France. Prutner also restores the mechanical movements of complicated watches.
22, rue de l'Échiquier, 75010 Paris
Tel.: + 33 (1) 48 24 02 15
Fax: + 33 (1) 48 24 12 96
E-mail: p.prutner@free.fr

Canada

● R.-J. RENAUD

Box 122, RR#1, Deep River,
Ontario, Canada K0J-1P0
Tel.: 613 584 3 744
E-mail: r.j.renaud@magma.ca

Australia

● ALLAN HEYWOOD ENAMELS

Restoration of enamel dials.
5 Montgomery St.
Skipton 3361
Tel. : + 613 (53) 40 2265
Web site: www.heywoodenamels.com
E-mail: allan@heywoodenamels.com

England

● FINE ANTIQUE CLOCKS

Derek Roberts carries a nice range of antique clocks dating from the seventeenth to the nineteenth centuries.
25 Shipbourne Road, Tonbridge, Kent,
TN10 3DN
Tel.: + 44 (1732) 35 89 86
Fax: + 44 (1732) 77 18 42
Web site: www.qualityantiqueclocks.com
E-mail: drclocks@clara.net

A watchmaker testing the movement of a perpetual calendar.

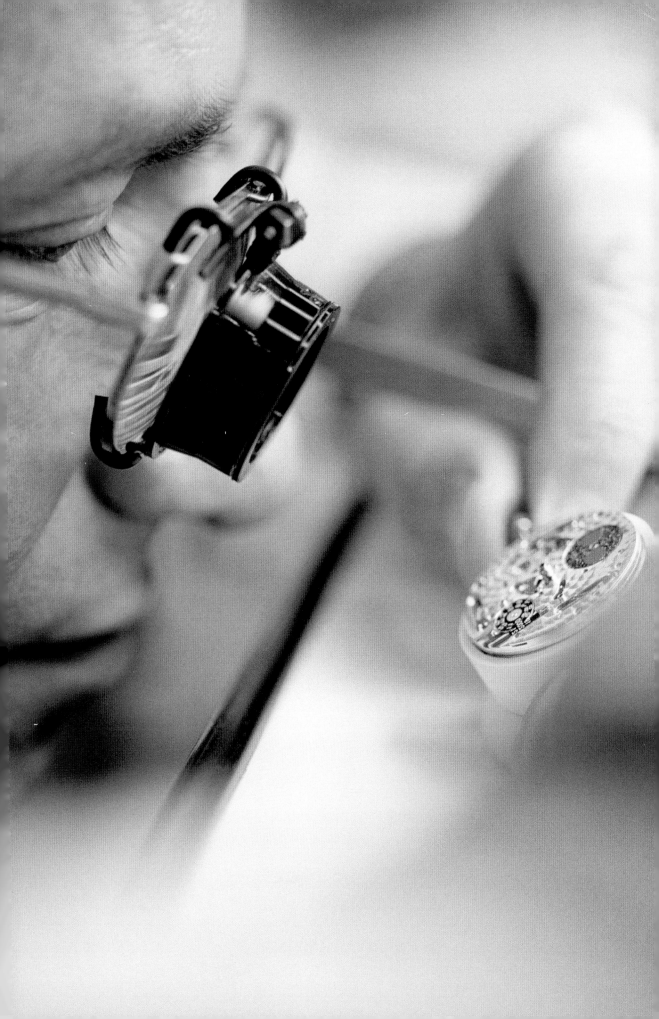

Collectible and secondhand watch specialists

France

● ROMAIN RÉA

This store carries an impressive selection of collectible watches, most of them made by the leading Swiss manufacturers. Romain Réa can also evaluate your models.

26, rue du Bac, 75007 Paris
Tel.: + 33 (1) 42 61 43 44
Fax: + 33 (1) 42 61 21 94
Web site: www.romainrea.com
E-mail: romainrea@noos.fr

● MMC

9, rue Marbeuf, 75008 Paris
Tel.: + 33 (1) 40 70 90 10
Fax: + 33 (1) 40 70 99 90
Web site: www.montres-modernes.com
E-mail: montres-modernes@wanadoo.fr

● ANTOINE DE MACEDO

46, rue Madame, 75006 Paris
Tel.: + 33 (1) 45 49 14 91
Fax: + 33 (1) 45 49 02 30
Web site: www.adm-horloger.com
E-mail: antoine-de-macedo@wanadoo.fr

● TIME GALLERY

6, allée Majorelle,
Le Louvre des Antiquaires,
2, place du Palais-Royal, 75001 Paris
Tel.: + 33 (1) 40 15 62 12
Fax: + 33 (1) 40 15 64 77
Web site: www.timegallery.fr
E-mail: info@timegallery.fr

● BROCANT'HEURE

Marché Dauphine aux puces, stand 233, 138, rue des Rosiers, 93558 Saint-Ouen
Tel. & Fax: + 33 (1) 40 12 27 02

● CRÉSUS

29, rue Gasparin, 69002 Lyon
Tel.: + 33 (4) 78 42 72 15
Fax: + 33 (4) 72 40 22 35
Web site: www.cresus.fr
E-mail: cresus2@wanadoo.fr

United States

● COOL VINTAGE WATCHES

Vintage 1900-1970 models by Breitling, Heuer, and Rolex.
5510 NE Antioch Rd., Kansas City, MO 64119
Tel.: 877 856 11 73
Fax: 00 (1) 816 436 5880
Web site: www.coolvintagewatches.com
E-mail: info@whattimeisit.net

● TOURNEAU

"The World's Largest Watch Store" is an authorized seller of many of the brands profiled in this book, as well as certified pre-owned watches and its own line, found at high-end shopping destinations throughout the United States.
Web site: www.tourneau.com